From the Pieces

an introduction to archaeology.

compiled by

Trevor F. Watkins

University of Edinburgh
Department of Archaeology
DIAMOND JUBILEE 1927-87

Contents

Acknowledgements

Like the exhibition to which it owes its origins, the contents of this book represent the work of many members of the Department of Archaeology. The illustrations were redrawn or adapted by Gordon Thomas assisted by Angela Wardell. The photographs were made or re-processed by Joe Rock and Trevor Cuthbert. The design and composition of the exhibition was by Gordon Thomas and Mrs Twin Watkins, and the organising group also included Ian Ralston, Trevor Watkins and chairman Roger Mercer.

In the production of the book Gordon Thomas played a special part in designing the cover, the illustrations and layout. Many colleagues have selflessly contributed material for adaptation and inclusion in the book; the way in which the material has been used, and the errors and misleading nuances which there will doubtless have been introduced, are the responsibility of the compiler. The Department was particularly grateful for the loan of material for the exhibition from the Anthropological Museum of Aberdeen University and the Base archaeologique du Mont Beuvray. It would be tedious to try to detail exactly the part of each of the many contributors to the exhibition and the book: it is better to list the names in alphabetic order. At the same time it is important to note that the field teams which carried out the work which is summarised here comprise many more names of students, graduates, and friends of the Department.

Material for the book and the exhibition was contributed by:–
Ian Armit, Alison Betts, Jane Blair, Clive Bonsall, Bill Finlayson, Joy Fulton, Stuart Campbell, Professor Dennis Harding, Roger Mercer, Magda Midgley, Eddie Peltenburg, Graham Philip, Carl Phillips, Ian Ralston, David Ridgway, Gordon Thomas, Richard Tipping, Trevor Watkins and Jenny Wilson.

The University of Edinburgh has provided funds and support for our research in many ways and from various funds, especially the General Council Trust. But by far the greater part of the funding was given by a host of different funding agencies. We are all glad to have this opportunity to acknowledge our great debt to all those bodies which have supported our recent work:–

Association for Cultural Exchange, Austrian Archaeological Institute, Cairo, Birmingham Museum and Art Gallery, British Academy, British Institute of Archaeology and History in Jordan, British Museum, British School of Archaeology in Iraq, British School of Archaeology in Jerusalem, Carnegie Trust for the Universities of Scotland, Central Research Fund of London University, Centre National de la Recherche Scientifique (ERA-314), Gordon Childe Bequest Fund, M. Aylwin Cotton Foundation, Cornwall Archaeological Society, Cumberland and Westmorland Antiquarian and Archaeological Society, Jennie S. Gordon Memorial Trust, Hanford Farms Ltd, Historic Buildings and Monuments Commission (English Heritage), Historic Buildings and Monuments Directorate (Scottish Development Department), Inveresk Research International, Margery Bequest Fund, Manpower Services Commission, Ministere de la Culture et de la Communication, Paris (Base archeologique du Mont Beuvray), National Geographic Society, National Museums of Scotland, Palestine Exploration Fund, Prehistoric Society, Royal Archaeological Institute, Russell Trust, Scottish Education Department, Society of Antiquaries of London, Society of Antiquaries of Scotland, State Organisation for the Antiquities and Heritage of Iraq, Royal Commission for the Ancient and Historical Monuments of Scotland, Geoffrey Averall Wainwright Fund.

FROM THE PIECES OF THE PAST

Preface

In October 1927 Vere Gordon Childe took up the newly
established Abercromby Chair of Prehistoric Archaeology in the
University of Edinburgh and began to teach undergraduate
students for an honours degree in the subject. Thus the academic
session 1987-88 represents the Diamond Jubilee of the first such
chair in a British university, and an important anniversary in the
recognition of archaeology within Britain as an independent
academic discipline.

To mark the occasion, there was an exhibition in the University
Library, and this book was produced along with the exhibition. The
exhibition was more concerned with the present, the future and
archaeology in general than with a retrospective view of the
Edinburgh Archaeology Department's history. It took a broad, view
of what archaeology can tell us about our human past. Taking the
image of a jigsaw puzzle, the exhibition was titled 'Piecing Together
the Past', which is also the title of one of Gordon Childe's own
books. The exhibition also illustrated through concrete examples
how archaeology contributes to the conservation and rescue,
interpretation and presentation of our cultural heritage, whether at
the Scottish, the national, or the international and world-wide level.

All the material in the main part of the exhibition was drawn from
work recently or currently in progress among students and staff in
the Edinburgh Department of Archaeology. The book takes the
same material and more. The exhibition was arranged in a series of
sections, which correspond to the sections in the book. Each section
takes a central theme of archaeological enquiry and illustrates how
that theme is pursued in research and what kinds of answers
archaeology can offer to our questions. Sometimes research projects
from very different parts of the world are put side by side in unlikely
juxtaposition to show how similar concerns motivate research
directed at the same goal but in often highly contrasted
environments. Instead of discussing the subject in theory or in
general, most of what the book has to say is put through the medium

of examples, particular pieces of research.

Like the exhibition, and like much archaeological research, the book draws upon the work of many hands. Although one hand has in the end written this text, it depends entirely on the contributions of many Edinburgh colleagues, who put together all the different elements which went to make up the exhibition. Their names are listed at the end of this section, and their unselfish help in the formation of this book is very gratefully acknowledged.

Of course, no one Department of Archaeology at any particular time happens to be carrying out research in every aspect of archaeology, or in every part of the world, or in every period of human history. On the other hand no introductory book could cover every aspect of archaeological enquiry; every book of this kind has to be highly selective. We have chosen to use our own work to illustrate our theme of 'Piecing Together the Past' for the obvious reason that the exhibition celebrated a very important milestone in the already long history of our Department.

For those who have seen the exhibition the book will tell you more, filling in some of the background to what you have seen and expanding on the themes which underlie the exhibition. But a book is less transient than an exhibition, and this book is intended to be able to stand on its own once the exhibition is finished. It is designed to serve as an introduction to what archaeology is about, what archaeologists are concerned with, and where archaeology relates to our everyday lives and the cultural world in which we live.

Introduction

Archaeology, like history, is concerned with the past. The historian utilises the documents of the past in order to interpret that past to himself and his readers of today. The archaeologist's documents are the surviving physical remains of the past, which are somewhat more difficult to 'read'. The most important contention of the archaeologist is that the unwritten record of the past can be read, and that, unlikely as it may seem at first thought, the record in pottery, buildings, weapons, graves is replete with information of use and interest to us on all aspects of human activity, thought and belief. Archaeology is no more escapism into a remote past than is history. It certainly is not just a technique for finding and collecting the curious but broken junk of the past. Over the years the ability of archaeology to reconstruct human affairs from the seemingly mute and meaningless fragments of the past, to 'read' the unwritten documents of the past, has developed greatly. In its concern with the interpretation of the physical remains of the historic heritage archaeology plays an important part in the national life. And in its deeper concern with the history and prehistory of human progress and social change over more than a million years and across the whole globe archaeology promotes unique insights into our own political, economic, and social lives, the human condition and our perception of it.

Before the reader embarks on the main body of this book, it is worth considering the special nature of the archaeological enquiry, which makes it such an absorbing and challenging subject for many people (and so frustrating for others). Pursuing the metaphor implied in the title, archaeology is a puzzlesolving or problemsolving subject, concerned with the jigsawlike pieces of the past. In the first place the raw materials of archaeology are literally the pieces of the past, sites of former settlement, graves and the remains of the dead, and all the bits and pieces with which people have surrounded themselves in their lives (and at their deaths).

It is a fundamental tenet of archaeology that people use things of all kinds in ways that relate extremely closely to every aspect of our lives. At one level things may be purely functional, tools which enable us to carry out our daily lives. In that sense it is indicative of our daily lives and what we do that one person may need a personal computer in the office and a sophisticated radio-telephone in the car, while someone else may use a spade and a rake as a gardener. In our society we all use ball-point pens, polythene bags, televisions, knives and forks, and paper bank-notes or plastic credit-cards: in other continents and in other contemporary societies, such things may be quite irrelevant, while other tools and equipment – perhaps bows and arrows, knives for butchery, digging sticks, and all sorts of other things quite unfamiliar to us – are regarded as absolutely essential.

But the things with which we surround ourselves are much more than just the tools of everyday life, much more subtle and multi-faceted than the 'purely functional'. We protect our bodies with clothes, which keep us warm and dry; but there is more to the clothes we wear than that. Clothes also protect our modesty; clothes may signify where we fit into our society, a sort of uniform which tells friends and strangers that we belong to this or that group, the armed forces or the yuppies, ageing flower-power or old fogeys, golfers, passe punks or sober-suited businessmen. We may wear a wrist-watch to help us to keep track of time, but it does not have to be gold, or to have three dials, or to have a Greek letter Omega on its face for that purpose: by all sorts of very subtle artefactual signifiers we give out messages to others and read messages about them. Archaeology is the theory and the skill of reading the messages implicit in things from the past.

To make the piecing together of the past more difficult we do not have all the pieces of the puzzle. For a variety of reasons many of the key pieces of the jigsaw are missing. Some of the pieces simply do not survive because the materials of which they were made soon decay in the soil. Some of the pieces are not available to us because they have not yet been found. Many of the pieces which we do have are in poor condition, broken, fragmentary or corroded – as if many of our jigsaw puzzle pieces had lost part of the picture on their surface. Archaeology refines mental torture in that it is like doing a jigsaw where we do not have all the pieces, some of the pieces are almost blank, and in addition we do not have the picture on the jigsaw puzzle box. Here the metaphor of the jigsaw puzzle breaks down. The end of the jigsaw puzzle is the satisfaction of putting the last piece into place and producing a facsimile of the picture on the box. In archaeology we can be sure that the puzzle is always incomplete; and the end is to recreate in the mind a best estimate of a past which once was there.

To return to the jigsaw puzzle metaphor for one further parallel, in archaeology we do not have the box with the picture on it, and all the pieces of the jigsaw are therefore scattered and lost. The first stage in the process of piecing together the past is to find some of the necessary pieces. The first section of this book is concerned with the recovery of information, that is the location of potentially informative spots in the landscape, their investigation and interpretation. Archaeologists call such parts of the landscape 'sites'. In theory a site is any place which has been the scene of human activity, but in practice it is defined as a focus of activity. A mountainside where once, ten thousand years ago, a hunter passed in pursuit of game is in theory a site, but in practice is not likely to have retained any perceptible trace of that activity. A temporary encampment, where hunters stopped to skin their kill and butcher it, or a village, or a city may be rich in information, and may be considered by an archaeologist as the most important site for the present purpose. Equally a cemetery, a factory, a rural shrine, some massive defensive system, or an area of former fields may constitute key sites for other purposes. Not only are such sites potentially useful to the archaeologist because they may yield tell-tale artefacts, but they are also artefacts in themselves, things made by human hands for human use and as informative as tools, clothes, weapons, ornaments, or any other kind of small, portable artefact. Equally a whole landscape may be a complex artefact, preserving traces of its former settlement and use, and allowing us an almost geographical perspective on the concept of the artefact.

The second section narrows down the focus to consider what kind of questions we may ask of settlements, the places where people have lived. At one level the place where we live will tell any investigator a good deal about the everyday routines of our life: at another level the place where we live can be read in the context of the society, economy and polity within which we live, and many of the messages are concerned with a good deal more than the routines of everyday existence.

The third section looks at artefacts, and considers how it is possible to analyse the things which people in the past have made and used. At the simplest level, to know what materials were in use, especially if one can tell where those materials came from, is a key to the basic economy of a society. Some communities may have been almost completely self-sufficient, while others (like our own) may have been heavily dependent on materials imported from elsewhere. Some communities possess almost all the skills necessary to make all the things which are necessary to their lives, but others (again like our own) may have been dependent on distant people for important manufactured goods. The analysis of artefacts can take place at many other levels of information; what level of technological skills were involved in manufacture, what functions did certain artefacts fulfil, and how effective were they, at what date was a certain kind of artefact in use, and can we use it for dating purposes, what culturally coded message did an artefact bear.

It may be fascinating to learn how a particular community obtained and used materials, or by what antique but nevertheless highly effective means it produced its basic foodstuffs, or to recover a technology (for example, flint-knapping) which was once commonplace but which is now all but lost to us. But what we also want to know about a past society is how it was ordered, how people viewed their world and what were their beliefs about how they fitted into the wider world. The web of social relationships may seem intangible, and even less concrete will be the ideas, views, beliefs which people shared, but, if the theory of archaeology is correct, human societies express themselves at all levels in an object-language, as well as in speech or writing.

It is a difficult task to move from what people did with their hands to what they thought and meant in their heads, but the clues are there in the concrete expressions of behaviour which survive for the archaeologist to explore and attempt to decode. The fourth section is directed at the examination of pieces of archaeological work which in different ways bear on the nature of a society or its shared beliefs.

The same section then goes on to consider another major aspect of the information potential of material remains from the past, its time-perspective. Archaeologists can be rather ambivalent on the question of chronology in their subject, especially if they are concerned with prehistoric times or a non-literate situation. Historians have laid down a chronological network, because so much of the documentary material which is the primary data of history is either directly dated or relatively dateable. The archaeologist working in a historical period, for example in a medieval town in Britain, or in the colonial period in North America, will rely on the historian's chronological framework. But when the archaeologist is working in an area and a period in which there is no historical chronology – and that of course applies to by far the greater part of man's history – then the necessary perspective on time must be discovered within the archaeological material itself. This task of discerning the time-dimension within archaeological sites or artefacts has been a major problem of great difficulty and a constant concern for almost two centuries, and archaeologists are sensitive about what some people is an unnatural obsession with the minutiae of chronology. Not even the advent of laboratory dating methods like radiocarbon dating, which has now been operational for at least thirty years, has changed matters very much: archaeologists still have considerable difficulty in the effective construction of the time-dimension in their work.

This difficulty with the time-perspective would be less important if time were not of the essence of much historical and archaeological enquiry. Indeed, the prehistoric perspective on time is enormous beyond contemplation. If the time-dimension can be fixed, archaeology can provide a matchless physical record of the major processes of human social, cultural and technical development over thousands and tens of thousands of years. The time-dimension, especially in prehistoric archaeology, is often much larger than is common in history. And the accounts of what was happening are very different in kind from those that we are accustomed to find in history books, simply because the stuff of archaeology is different from the stuff of history.

There are two reasons in particular why archaeology has an urgent and exciting air about it, and these are explored in Section 6. Archaeology is still an adolescent discipline when compared to history, the study of the classics or the natural sciences. Over the last half century archaeological theory, methods and techniques have changed dramatically. As a subject with a strong technical aspect, archaeology is constantly taking advantage of new technological and scientific applications of all kinds. There are new methods of physical analysis, new laboratory methods of dating, new and amazing surveying instruments, and of course the almost universal micro-computer. All these technical applications open new possibilities for getting more information and novel kinds of information. Along with the technical innovations come new theoretical and conceptual views, which transform and enlarge the way we can encounter our human past.

The other aspect of archaeology where there is always something new, something exciting, something quite unexpected which requires the textbooks to be re-written, is the frequent discovery of previously unknown cultural worlds. After all, since the potential scope of archaeology covers the whole of human history over the whole globe, and since archaeological field research has been under way for only about one hundred years since the time of Schliemann at Troy, Petrie in Egypt or Pitt-Rivers in England, it is hardly surprising that there are still huge virgin territories to be explored. Even where exploration has been going on for a long time, as for example in Britain, there are still surprises, still parts of the country about which almost nothing is known.

The last section of the book looks at the public face of archaeology. For at least a hundred years, some archaeologists, from General Pitt-Rivers, through Sir Mortimer Wheeler, have been aware of the importance of archaeology's relations with the public and the state. For the student whose selection of archaeology as a subject of study is a personal choice, for the academic archaeologist in a university whose work is still officially and quaintly referred to as 'private research', for the interested amateur and member of a local society, it may seem on the face of it inconsequential that archaeology has a public place. However, the public face of archaeology and the role of the state in archaeology have become increasingly important matters, not least because in most countries most of the professional archaeologists and much of the largerscale archaeological work done are funded from the public purse.

The two particular issues which are taken up in this final section are archaeology as intervention and archaeology as interpretation. There is frequently a need for archaeological intervention in order to record sites and salvage information when there is a damaging conflict of interests between unique but fragile remains of the past and contemporary requirements of re-development, mechanised agriculture, afforestation, hydro-electric power, improved communications systems and much else. Our human historical and cultural heritage has left its traces in our landscape, whether they are easy to recognise (like Edinburgh Castle, Hadrian's Wall or Westminster Abbey) or forgotten and unknown. The environment in which we live, and whose quality is being recognised as being of great importance to the quality of our lives, is in part an historical environment. And the debates about the line of a new motor-way, the intensification of agriculture, the afforestation of unproductive land, are all debates about the archaeological and historical environment as much as about the natural environment.

The second theme in the last section, archaeology as interpretation, is explored in terms of the public's need or demand for interpretation. It is self-evident that archaeologists, whether paid professionals or independents and amateurs, will find the implications of what they have discovered fascinating, but what is the value to the public of these discoveries? As tourism, museums, visitor and interpretation centres burgeon, and TV documentaries and popular publishing still flourish, what is the interface between academic, intellectual and highly technical archaeology and the public appreciation of the past?

There are many other aspects of the public face of archaeology which are not considered here, just as there are other very important aspects of archaeology which are not discussed in other chapters. As was said at the beginning of this introduction, the book, like the exhibition, is necessarily highly selective. We have also been concerned to produce something different. The exhibition has sought to make a statement about archaeology in general, about how we can seek to piece together our human past, whereas most archaeological exhibitions are devoted to something specific, like 'The Chinese Warriors', 'Symbols of Power', or 'Treasures of the ---

National Museum'.

The book also sets out to be an introduction to archaeology which is different from other books of this kind (which are many, and many of them good). The particular difference in this book is that it tackles the job primarily by means of illustrative example rather than by means of theoretical discussion or practical and technical explication. All archaeological work is conditioned by the basic factors of the incomplete and accidental nature of archaeological data and the means at our disposal for locating, obtaining, recording and analysing primary data.

This is perhaps where the paradox of archaeology lies, which makes it importantly different from most other subjects with which people are more or less familiar. Archaeology is different from other subjects in the area of the arts and humanities, whose data is primarily the written word; yet it is also different from the natural and environmental sciences, with which it shares so much in terms of the raw materials of its data. Archaeology, like the arts, humanities and social sciences, is centrally concerned with the greater understanding of human activity, behaviour and thought. But the physical nature of archaeological data requires archaeologists to treat, classify and analyse that data in ways that have more in common with the physical and environmental sciences. From the experience of teaching archaeology at the introductory level over a number of years and to a variety of groups, it seems useful to make the nature and limitations of archaeological data and our available means of int errogating that data the central and constant themes.

Section 1: Landscape with distant figures

The plan in the first part of this book is to start at the largest scale and work down to the smallest. Thus we begin with landscapes and work on through the next section on settlements to the third section on the pottery, metal objects and other kinds of artefacts which people make and use. The question to be discussed is what have archaeologists learned that they can find out from such things, whether they are landscapes, sites or the ultimate bric-a-brac of broken pottery or corroded iron fragments. The text of this section (and that of the following sections, too) is punctuated by examples which illustrate the points by means of reference to specific research projects.

For any of us who do not live in a wilderness the landscape around us will be full of signs of the history of its human use over many centuries. A typical townscape might perhaps contain a school, which may take the form of an institutional-style building of the early part of this century rather poorly suited to today's changed educational ideas, areas of industrial buildings, some of which may be a century and more old and much modified over the intervening decades, some elegant and spacious town-houses of considerable antiquity, but now used as offices, and an even more ancient parish church. A typical rural landscape might perhaps contain farm-buildings of ages ranging from the most modern sectional metal barns to a house which was originally a medieval hall, a field-system some of whose hedges go back many centuries, perhaps an 18th century canal, a 19th century railway line, and even a Roman road. Concealed within and below those landscapes will be many other traces of the past. In order to make any sense of the historical landscape we need to be able to look at it with the added dimension of time; and we also need to recover as much of any historical landscape as we can , rather than be content with the few fragments which stand up and hit us in the eye.

What we can hope to learn from any historical or archaeological landscape is just the same as the historical geographer would hope to discover in the spatial organisation of human life and activity at a particular period. But in order to restore a map of a particular past landscape it is necessary to ensure that it is as representative and complete as possible. Even in areas of Britain, which is and has been relatively densely populated, and which has been as well explored in historical and archaeological terms as any country, there are still large areas of landscape which have not yet been systematically searched for historical and prehistoric remains.

In very few parts of the world is it possible to pick up a ready-made map of settlement for any particular period. It might be thought that at least the Roman military map of the northern frontier in Scotland, the line of the Antonine Wall and its associated works, was well enough known after so much investigation over such a long time; after all, the physical traces of the Roman occupation of Scotland have been recognised and the focus of interest for over three hundred years. Nevertheless, there are still crucial gaps in the map, and from year to year new military camps and even new forts are discovered.

In those parts of the landscape which have remained in agricultural use most surface traces of the former existence of abandoned farms, deserted villages and the other components of an ancient landscape may have been gradually smoothed away. In towns and cities the remains of the medieval and earlier town may lie below the pavements, the shops and offices of the modern city centre. But in many other parts of the landscape fragments at least of earlier landscapes have survived on the surface to be seen by any who have eyes to see. As is so often the case, the difficulty is in seeing and recognising what one is looking at: t he eye needs to be trained and attuned.

Soon after the First World War of 1914 to 1918, using the wartime experience of flying for airborne observation, a few pioneers began to recognise that not only could one profit archaeologically from a bird's eye view, but that the evidence could be photographed and recorded. Aircraft, cameras and photographic emulsions have been very much improved over the intervening years, but a slow-flying light aircraft at low altitude is still the best vehicle for aerial survey. There are three circumstances which allow archaeological remains which cannot be appreciated at ground level to be seen from the air. Where there is still some physical relief on the ground surface, this may be amplified and clarified by being viewed from an altitude of several hundred metres when a low winter sun strikes across it. A particularly chilly adaptation of the raking winter sun principle which has yielded very dramatic photographic results is that of flying early in the morning after fairly light snow has been blown across the landscape by a strong wind, or as the early morning sun begins to melt a thick hoar frost.

Where archaeological remains have been completely flattened there may still be clear traces to be observed and recorded from the air either in the plough-soil itself or in the crop growing. In these conditions, that is with soil-marks and crop-marks, what is seen on the surface reflects sub-surface details, sometimes in quite remarkable detail. Soil-marks are quite simply the effect of the plough bringing to the surface differently coloured and textured material from the tops of buried ditches, walls or roads. Crop-marks are a good deal more mysterious, for the same field can produce different images from year to year. In general, crop-marks are the differences in the colour of a crop, typically a cereal, because of differences in the moisture available to its roots. The critical period is when the crop is beginning to mature and change colour. It is also necessary to have a free-draining subsoil such as sand or gravel. Then, especially if there is also a dry period to amplify the differences between drying subsoil and moisture-retentive soils in ancient pits and ditches, plants growing in drying soil will ripen more quickly while plants whose roots are fed by the moister soils will remain greener and darker.

So much for the means of gathering information; how can it be used? In the first place the photogmation from aerial survey has to be transcribed on to standard maps. The archaeological remains found on ground surveys likewise need to be surveyed and planned and the information, drawings, photographs and written descriptions, needs to be catalogued and mapped. How the ordered information can now be used depends in part on the purpose for which it was collected. Some survey work consists of putting together and verifying information about sites which are already known to exist in a particular area, simply to produce a 'sites and monuments register', a basic database for administrative purposes. Primary field survey, searching an area for evidence of archaeological remains, is either very time-consuming or labour-intensive.

In Britain, to take the obvious example, four Royal Commissions on Ancient Monuments (one each for England, Scotland, Wales and Northern Ireland) have been at work since the early years of this century inventorising the ancient and historical sites and monuments. To date the work is incomplete, and meanwhile, of course, the early inventories are themselves becoming historical documents. The highly expert staff of the Royal Commissions are very small in number, and their painstaking work is carried out to the highest standards. Ideally, their inventories should supply the database for almost any kind of subsequent work on the historic or prehistoric landscapes of Britain. In fact their statutory purpose is to provide information and recommendations to Government to enable it to decide what sites and monuments among all the rest should be given legal protection. The Royal Commission's task in an uphill struggle, for their resources are strictly limited, and their earliest county inventories are now long out of date while some important parts of the country still await primary survey.

Intensive but immediate surveys of particular areas are constantly needed, for example in response to the serious threat of extensive afforestation, which can very rapidly engulf very large areas of thinly populated landscape. It should not be thought that because an area now has an almost non-existent level of population it has always been so. Large tracts of the Scottish highlands were massively depopulated at the 'Clearances'; but almost nothing may be known of the immediately pre-Clearance and earlier landscapes. Few archaeologists, historians and local societies have worked in the remote highlands. Edinburgh University Archaeology Department teams of as many as twenty people under the direction of Roger Mercer worked on intensive surveys of areas of Caithness which were about to be forested. Large amounts of information were there to be recorded, ranging in date from huge, complex neolithic burial cairns five thousand years old to the crofts, farm-touns and fields which were abandoned at the Clearances only a couple of centuries ago. The new forestry can avoid wrecking the more important sites, if the archaeologists can indicate where they are; and the total survey of thousands of hectares of land has provided a wealth of research data on the former settlement, which is now under investigation.

The potential of the information recovered by survey is often difficult to realise because of the problems of introducing a time dimension into the evidence. It is essential to be able to recognise what elements on the map belong together; and it would be completely misleading to inter-relate sites whose inhabitants could no have known each other because they lived at different times. Sometimes people were kind enough to leave chronological indicators lying about for archaeologists to find. In the Near East, for example, pottery was in very common use (and very commonly broken, too) over the last eight thousand years. By means of careful excavation archaeologists have been able to learn at what dates certain styles of pottery were current. And pottery is a great boon to archaeologists since pottery is relatively fragile and of no use once broken, and fired clay survives in almost any soil conditions. The eroded mounds which represent the remains of mud-brick settlements over large areas of the Near and Middle East are littered with broken pottery which is a tell-tale indicator of the periods when the settlement was in occupation.

In other cases the sites themselves may be indicative of their date. The ditches of Roman temporary camps, for example, can be readily identified in aerial survey because of the characteristic playing-card plan of Roman military works. In the case of the Plym Valley survey in Dartmoor National Park (see the picture-story in the last chapter), the date of the tin workings is assumed because the industrialisation of tin production is historically documented. The remarkably early date of the extensive settlement and associated farming of Dartmoor was possible because other archaeologists had recently shown by excavation that such little villages of stone-built houses and the division of the landscape into broad territories and small fields do indeed date around 1000 B.C.

Clearly, if three thousand years ago there was a good scattering of farming villagers and enclosed fields across what is now a wild, open landscape like Dartmoor, environmental conditions are surely different now from then. Similarly, environmental conditions in the Jordanian Black Desert (see the account of the survey below) were surely somewhat kinder to hunters than they are now if that inhospitable area was once inhabited. Similarly, in the aerial survey of the Scottish southern uplands, defended enclosures on high hill-tops can be seen to be surrounded by their arable fields at altitudes well beyond the reach of modern, high-tech agriculture. Was the climate different then? Or were there subtle factors which made the environment then more amenable than it appears now? Was it man himself who wrought the changes?

The best available indicators of climate and of local environmental conditions are ancient soils and particularly contemporary plant remains. The difficulty with identifying ancient soils is in isolating a soil which has not been subject to addition or change since the time in which one is interested. What the archaeologist and the soil scientist will be looking for is a buried soil, for example, under a hill-fort rampart or a burial mound. A buried soil may be capable of indicating something of the climatic conditions under which it was formed, and will certainly be able to tell the soil scientist whether the ground was forested or open.

Plant remains can be equally difficult to locate on an ancient site. Organic materials will only survive under certain, specialised conditions, such as extreme aridity (for example in the tombs of ancient Egypt, which were always located in the desert edges above the Nile valley), or conversely waterlogging (as in the lake-edge sites which were discovered in Switzerland in the 19th century, or in the wetland sites being excavated in the Somerset peat-levels or the Fens of East Anglia). Alternatively, plant parts which have been carbonised into charcoal will survive in most soil conditions. In the case of plant remains recovered in Egyptian tombs, though, as with the carbonised seeds and wood fragments from any settlement site, it has to be remembered that what we have is a view of some of the plants which were in use, not necessarily a diagnostic cross-section of the plant-species best calculated to portray the nature of the environment. Indeed, the plant remains on a site may be as exotic as the foodstuffs in any of our homes, and quite unrepresentative of the local environmental conditions. This was the case, for example, at the Roman fort at Bearsden in Glasgow, where sewage had been

14

allowed to accumulate in the bottom of a ditch. The seeds of exotic fruits had been preserved in the waterlogged ditch, and showed that the Roman military needed to be supplied with foodstuffs to which they were accustomed no less than United States NATO forces need their PX.

One of the most surprising sources of information about the former nature of an area is to be found in pollen. While pollen is so microscopically small and light that it can float in the air (and cause many of us hayfever), it is far from fragile. Pollen grains have a silica shell and pollen can survive more or less indefinitely, especially in wet conditions such as lake beds or peat-bogs. The pollen grains of each plant species are as distinctive under the microscope as the flowers or the leaves. Where they are found in quantity not only can the different species which once grew in the neighbourhood be identified, but the relative proportions of the species to one another in the landscape can be calculated. In addition, locations such as peat-bogs or shallow lake-beds tend to accumulate over time, so that the pollen is nicely stratified. Given fortunate circumstances and a great deal of work it is possible to reconstruct the vegetation history of a region over hundreds and thousands of years. Of course it still remains to tie the archaeological remains in which one is interested to the pollen spectrum of the same date. That is most easily done by obtaining radiocarbon dates for the stratified peat in order to identify which part of a column of peat is the critical one.

The survey data on its own, even when it is plentiful and the map seems excitingly dense, is nevertheless only a specialised form of map. It no more tells us what people were doing and how their political, economic or social world was organised than does a modern map of our contemporary world. All depends upon our ability to interpret the static formulae of the two-dimensional map in terms of the dynamics of people's lives. We can use the techniques which geographers use for interpreting modern maps, for example central place theory or Thiessen polygons, as long as we can be confident that the contemporary conditions which the geographical method is intended to interpret existed in the ancient landscape which we are seeking to reveal. Central place theory, which has been employed quite often in archaeology, was devised to explain the spatial relationships of 20th century, post-Industrial Revolution economic activity; the application of this type of analysis to a map of the past has to be carefully thought through, since it would be dangerous to assume that the same assumptions will apply in exactly the same way.

In almost every analysis of a landscape we shall need to know more about individual settlements within it than we can observe on the ground or from the air. It will be necessary to probe below the surface, to undertake in-depth analysis of selected sites. Excavation is a basic archaeological tool for exploring individual sites, and in the next section we shall concentrate on the question of how archaeologists use excavation to obtain information about settlements.

Aerial survey in Scotland

One (but only one) of the contributions made by aerial survey is in the discovery of new archaeological sites. A crew consisting of a pilot, archaeologist/mapreader and photographer in a light aircraft can quarter a very considerable territory in a single sortie. On the other hand aerial survey is an expensive activity; it is not only that flying is costly, but also that high-quality cameras are needed, and over a season the costs of film and the processing of film are not inconsiderable. The aerial surveyors will make careful preparations to ensure as far as possible that they fly at times and in areas where their presence will be productive.

Another important aspect of aerial survey work is the repetition of visits to areas where sites are known in the hope of capturing additional information. It may seem improbable to those who have not seen aerial photographs of the same site at different times that some visual information may appear for only a few days, fade, and be replaced by other information. Information observed on one visit may be quite invisible in another year; but new information never previously noted may by the same token be seen for the first time on a site which has been known and watched for several years. The reasons for this unpredictability are only in part understood as yet.

One of several programmes of aerial survey under way at present in Scotland is that undertaken in Grampian Region by a partnership of an academic archaeologist and the archaeologist employed by the regional authority. Their work is in part funded by the Royal Commission on the Ancient and Historical Monuments of Scotland. The Royal Commission have an interest in recording sites throughout Scotland; the regional authority is concerned to have a record of the sites within its own grossly under-prospected area, and the university archaeologist regards the survey as a means of undertaking research into the historic and prehistoric settlement patterns of a geographically very diverse region.

There are two types of surface information which can be read from the air. Colour differences in crops, other vegetation and soil may betray sub-surface features on an otherwise flat field. In areas which have remained unploughed since they were last occupied there may still be surface relief, perhaps undetectable at ground level. Seen from the altitude of an aircraft under the right lighting conditions, even the slightest variations in the surface of the ground may stand out. A

17

Fig 1. Low sun and snow reveal an ancient landscape at Wardhouse, Grampian Region.

low, raking light across the landscape is needed to show up such minimal 'humps and bumps'. Alternatively, if the surveyors are willing to fly with the side-window open early on a winter morning after a dusting of snow has been air-blown across the hills, or as the sun rises on a deep hoar frost, they may be rewarded with a view of almost incredible surface detail.

In the southern uplands of Scotland, for example, it is not uncommon to be able to observe evidence for the ploughing of fields in prehistoric times. Even the ring-like depressions left in the turf where timbers set in a circular foundation trench once supported the conical roof of a house can be seen and recorded on film. Another programme of aerial survey and research in Scotland has been directed at the late prehistoric settlement of the southern uplands of Scotland. The main fortified settlements of the first millennium B.C. were quite well known in general terms, but aerial survey has revealed a great deal more detail and also that large tracts of land around some of these windy hill-top settlements were under arable cultivation. More sorties were flown as an adjunct of the Bowmont Valley survey (see later in this section) to produce a finer degree of detail than was visible on the standard vertical air-photo archive.

It is equally important to be in the right place at the right time to catch the second type of information. Cropmarks appear only in certain soil conditions, and only in certain weather conditions. When the circumstances are right, there may appear a pattern of extraordinary detail showing as darker strips and patches in the ripening crop. On occasions even the individual postholes dug to house the timber uprights of the frame of a house can be distinguished five thousand years after the timber house has gone. Just such a large timber building was seen and photographed at Balbridie (see the later section on the experimental reconstruction of the excavated house remains) on Deeside in N. E. Scotland as part of the systematic survey of areas of gravel subsoil in the river valleys.

There are two technical difficulties which are brought about by the very success of systematic aerial survey, and once again it is the micro-computer which is being brought to the rescue. When aerial photographs contain a wealth of coherent detail, it is natural to wish to transfer the data to the map and translate it into accurate two-dimensional form. However, the camera was almost never directly vertical over the cropmark, and it is difficult and cumbersome to compensate for the obliquity in the photograph. Now there are computer programs which make all the necessary compensations and draw the result at any scale. The operator uses a digitiser to put the cropmark data into the computer's memory, and identifies a few key points, such as the corners of fields, which are common to the photograph and the map. The computer can then take care of the rest of the task for itself; and it can also store the digitised image it has redrawn for later review.

The second technical difficulty has been the revision of the plans transcribed from aerial photographs in the light of new information. Here again the microcomputer is beginning to prove itself invaluable. The computer can handle images almost as readily as it can handle text or numbers. Having transcribed and rectified the information from one photograph, the computer can draw it and store it. The stored image can be brought out for comparison with another version taken from a different photograph of the same site. And the researcher can combine the elements of both into a third, composite picture. In this way the computer is used as the keeper of the archive of transcribed images; and it also allows the operator to work up the best composite version and store that for future reference.

The Black Desert, Jordan.

Wilderness, like beauty, is often in the eye of the beholder. Areas which are now very thinly populated by contrast with the dense urban landscapes in which many of us live may be called desert, but they nevertheless carry a human population and they may contain the traces of a surprising, unfamiliar and informative history.

The Black Desert in eastern Jordan is a spectacularly desolate wasteland of ancient lava flows, now eroded out into a boulder-strewn landscape, punctuated by stretches of stark, white mudflats. The only wild animals in the area today are snakes, mice, lizards, scorpions and some small game, such as hare and sand grouse. Until the last century there were many larger animals, in particular ostrich, oryx, wild ass and large herds of gazelle. Predators once included lions and leopard, but now there are only wild dogs and hyenas. Clearly, the Black Desert was formerly a richer landscape than it appears today. The evidence suggests that man's activities have made the environment poorer, rather than that climatic factors are responsible.

Despite its (to us) barren appearance the Black Desert has been used by nomadic groups since earliest times. The land has never been settled or cultivated, and so prehistoric sites and their accompanying tool scatters remain almost exactly as they were left thousands of years ago.

Working in an area such as the Black Desert poses practical problems. Survey work must be done in the dry season when temperatures are very high, and the rockstrewn landscape is impassable to vehicles, which means that most work must be carried out on foot. To make the task of the ground surveyor easier much of the preliminary investigation is done through study of aerial photographs and maps. Satellite imagery shows landforms and the larger archaeological sites, while medium level air photography from aircraft can be used to locate most structures. For making detailed plans of buildings and other constructions low level air photography with a camera suspended from a kite or a balloon is very helpful.

Most of the people who use the Black Desert today move through the basalt only seasonally. They are beduin from villages to the west of the desert who move out with their flocks in winter in order to make

Fig 2. *Landscape with distant figure in the Black Desert: in the foreground the ruined stone wall os a settlement, and beyond the walls of 'kite' enclosures.*

use of the flush of fresh grazing. This is probably a pattern of great antiquity which may have begun some seven thousand years ago, when the first nomadic pastoralists appeared in the area. Only sheep and goat are herded in the Black Desert as the rocky landscape is unsuitable for camels.

Before the pastoralists there were hunters. They used the rocks of the desert surface to build vast chains of animal traps into which they drove herds of gazelle. Animals grazing on the mudflats would be surprised and driven up a hill, guided by low walls into a small enclosure below the brow of the hill. Here more hunters would be lying in wait to shoot the animals trapped in the enclosure. While watching for the herds to appear, the hunters would sometimes sit on a hill-top vantage point, using the time to flake flint and prepare their arrowheads. Their flint debris can still be found, as are the massive remains of their traps, giving evidence of a way of life which was practised about eight thousand years ago.

Before that again there were other hunters, who used less specialised strategies. At that period, about ten thousand years ago, hunting groups made seasonal camps in the north of the area, where the rainfall is very slightly higher. They hunted a variety of small game, but also depended to a greater degree on wild plant foods. To process the seeds which they harvested they pounded them in deep mortars cut into the natural basalt bedrock.

All of these human groups over ten thousand years have left traces of their fleeting activities in the form of their camps, their traps, their tools, their discarded debris and their rock-carvings. The evidence of their passing lies undisturbed on the surface, awaiting the archaeologist who maps and investigates the sites. What emerges is a surprisingly rich story of how this arid environment has been exploited over many millennia in different ways by hunters and pastoralists.

Bowmont Valley, Borders Region, Southern Scotland

The River Bowmont rises high in the Cheviot Hills hard against the border with England, and flows first north and then east to become a tributary of the famous River Tweed. In its first ten miles the river and its feeder streams run in steep- sided valleys cut into the Cheviots. The country is high and wild. Until recently the valley has been one of the principal upland routes across the border between Kelso and Harbottle in Northumberland; indeed, 'H' for Harbottle can still be seen on the 18th century milestones that stand beside one of the tracks that cross the border. The traffic in the border areas, however, was not always peaceable, and the Bowmont Valley saw its fair share of the turbulent history of the English-Scottish Border.

The upper part of the valley, an area of approximately 10 miles long by 4 miles wide, was recently exhaustively surveyed in advance of the development of forestry and more intensive grazing. Although the landscape is presently very thinly populated, there were many traces of its former, denser inhabitation and use. The archaeologists had the chance to intervene and rescue the richly detailed pages of the former history and prehistory of this landscape before the planned new use eradicates those traces once and for all. For hundreds of years the principal economic activity in the area has been the running of sheep, an activity which causes minimal damage to the physical traces of earlier forms of landscape use. Thus the Bowmont Valley preserved an imprint of the successive phases of man's inhabitation in and utilisation of the landscape over many centuries.

Although aerial photographs tend to suppress the general relief of the landscape, the detailed imprints of human activity were extraordinarily clear. For this survey the procedure was to enlarge the earliest series of available RAF aerial photographs (the 1947 series preserves details which have been removed by recent farming), transfer the information to maps, and then to investigate and map the remains on the ground.

There were three kinds of remains, the traces of human settlement, the traces of cultivation, and the ribbons of routeways passing through the landscape.

Perhaps the most unexpected of these elements were the traces of cultivation, but the remains were unambiguous; at various times in

23

the distant past communities living in the valley practised arable agriculture. In the steep-sided valleys careful terracing and drainage had to be constructed; terracing is visible on the valley slopes up to altitudes of about 330 metres (1000 feet). At lower altitudes the corrugations of 'rig and furrow' cultivation were to be found. Usually at higher altitudes than the rig and furrow patterns, there were also small, vestigial patches of a much narrower pattern of rig and furrow, which archaeologists have dubbed 'cord rig'. Because one mode of cultivation will inevitably obliterate traces of an earlier form, it is possible to see in the landscape how these three arable cultivation modes are to be arranged in sequence: the cord rig is the earliest, followed by the cultivation terraces; the broader rig and furrow which is so extensive at the lower altitudes is the most recent pattern of cultivation to have been added to the scene.

Drove-roads wound their way along the ridges up the valley towards the watershed at the English border, forming a corridor of communication across the landscape under survey. Sometimes they appear as sunken trackways, worn deeply into the landscape, while in other places they braid into multiple courses where herders and animals tackled the steeper gradients or the mud-clogged hollows. The droving of cattle to distant markets has been an age-old feature of Scottish history. Taking cattle through a valley where arable crops were widely grown must have led to longstanding conflicts of interest between the resident farmers and the drovers and herds passing through; there are the remains of earthworks bounding droveways and protecting the arable areas, and the survey shows that the droveways up the valley are at least as old as the oldest phase of cultivation.

Scattered through the landscape of cultivation, where later cultivation itself has not erased them, lie the remains of the settlements of the people who lived in the valley in earlier times. There is a considerable variety of form and size of settlement, and within settlements it is possible to see different plans of house, and changes of size or construction method, which presumably reflect different social, economic and cultural conditions at different periods. There is both internal and external evidence which makes it possible to discern the chronological perspective of changing settlement patterns in the valley over long periods of time. Internally, it is sometimes possible to observe that a certain type of settlement was embedded within a particular type of arable cultivation. The dating of house types or settlement types which have been excavated elsewhere in south-east Scotland can sometimes be imported into the valley, when similar and distinctive houses or settlements are recognised in the survey. Although no excavation has taken place, it is nevertheless possible to sketch a long and varied history of settlement and land-use in the upland Bowmont Valley in terms of six periods.

Fig 3.   Hayhope Knowe shows a complex series of round houses, palisade, dump rampart and 'cord-rig' agriculture.

Phase 1. The earliest occupation was deep in prehistoric times, yet nevertheless it seems to have been substantial in scale. External dating would suggest that this initial phase of occupation by villages of arable farmers should be dated to the early centuries of the first millennium B.C. The settlements were villages of circular houses arranged on either side of a street. Each settlement was enclosed within a tall fence or palisade of timber, and the amounts of timber required to build the quite substantial houses and the very substantial palisades imply that considerable land clearance was necessary and plenty of forest was removed. The palisades around settlements may well have been intended to keep cattle and other animals out of the settlement area as much as for defence.

Phase 2. The large, circular houses of the previous phase generally increase in size in the second phase, up to 12 metres and more in diameter. In this second phase settlements often continue where they were, but the number of houses which comprise a settlement is usually much smaller, often only two or three. In some cases it is possible to see that the palisade which had enclosed the earlier settlement was removed or allowed to decay. It may also be during the course of this phase that a number of settlements were built on hill-top sites, enclosed by a stone-built rampart. The original wall might then be reinforced in time by multiple encircling ditches. Elsewhere houses of the distinctive form of this phase have been dated to around 500 B.C. Perhaps the appearance of defended hill-top settlements and their increasing concentration on defence denote a crisis which led to the demise of the Phases 1 and 2 settlement pattern.

Phase 3. It is thought that a newly discovered series of small, circular houses, no more than 6 metres in diameter, mark the next phase in the history of settlement in the valley. These new settlements are formed of groups of about half a dozen such houses, and they are particularly distinctive for the way that each house is set on a platform scooped out of the slope.

Phase 4 is the period of scooped settlements within earthen enclosures. Each farmstead comprises some three to five small, circular, cell-like houses set around a yard area within a massive, quarried scoop in the hill-side. Around the rim of the scoop is a considerable rampart. From similar settlements excavated south of the border in Northumberland it would appear that such enclosed farmstead date to the centuries immediately prior to the arrival of the Roman legions in north Britain, and they probably continued through the early centuries A.D.

It was during this period that the extensive cultivation of the valley by means of agricultural terraces took place, for it is possible to see that some scooped farmsteads fit into areas of terracing, which neither over-runs the sites nor is curtailed to allow the farmsteads to be built.

Phase 5 can be pinned down by documentary evidence to the 12th century A.D., when thriving villages existed at 'Mow' or Mowhaugh and at Attonburn ('Auld town burn'). These settlements can be seen to be at the focus of their own rig and furrow agriculture. Although the older pattern of agricultural terraces can sometimes be detected overlain by rig and furrow, thereby confirming the chronological sequence, the medieval rig and furrow systems were never so extensive as the older agriculture.

These farming villages are mentioned in contemporary documents because they were the subjects of squabbles between monasteries concerned for their territorial rights. It is also known that the monasteries like that at Kelso, which managed its rights in the Bowmont Valley through a grange farms such as Elieshaugh, were introducing sheep-farming to the area. Arable agriculture certainly continued, but the change to sheep-farming received a major push in the period of agricultural improvements of the early 19th century.

Phase 6 is marked by the building in the 1860's by the Roxburgh Estates (lineal successors in land-rights to the monks of Kelso) of a series of model farms at Mowhaugh, Attonburn and Cliftoncote. It is only very recently, in the 1970's and 1980's, that the building layout of these farms is itself becoming obsolete in the face of the new 'industrialisation' of British farming.

Although a good deal of the history of settlement and land-use in the valley over almost three thousand years can be read in the surface of the ground, further information could be gained only by highly specific and economical excavation projects. The minute examination of the aerial photographs and the surveying of over 600 sites of archaeological interest in the valley has unfolded the general outlines and laid the basis for choosing how and where future excavation might take place. Field survey can thus be seen as serving the present need of salvaging information from a drastically changing landscape, and at the same time indicating the research strategies of the future.

Wadi al Qawr, Ras al Khaimah, United Arab Emirates

By the third millennium B.C. there was an economically powerful urban civilization in southern Mesopotamia, modern S. Iraq, the early forerunner of the famous Babylonian civilization. Its extensive irrigation systems allowed it to produce a massive food surplus, but it was devoid of certain raw materials essential to the economy (such as metals) or for the manufacture of equally essential luxury and symbolic items (such as precious metals, precious stones, unguents, special timbers). Texts of the period from the Mesopotamian cities boast of the extent of their trade, and mention in particular the ships and merchants who came from faraway places down the Gulf.

Around 1960 the island of Bahrain began to be identified with the centre of the mysterious ancient civilization of Dilmun, known for more than a century from the Mesopotamian texts as an important entrepot for trade between Mesopotamia and points further southeast, places such as Magan and Meluhha. It now appears likely that Magan may have been modern Oman and S. E. Arabia, while Meluhha may be the Indus Valley urban civilization, spread over much of the N. W. Indian sub-continent. Only in the 1970's did it become possible for archaeologists to begin work in E. and S. E. Arabia.

The archaeology of these areas had received almost no previous attention, and our knowledge of the ancient world of Arabia and the Gulf is still in its infancy, but, like a little child, growing at an exciting rate. Set within such a framework of major urban civilizations and long-distance trade by sea from such an early date, the eastern side of the Arabian peninsula presents a major challenge to our historical and archaeological enterprise. As well as size the Arabian peninsula possesses great variety of environment, and some natural resources, such as copper, which were of major international importance. Much of the first archaeological work in the area was concentrated on the coastal and oasis environments, but it is becoming clear that there was much more extensive settlement, and that the external forces worked upon local cultures which were quite distinctive and were not to be understood simply as responses to the economic demands of distant urban centres. Over the millennia, and within such a complex set of long-distance relations, one could expect that the history of the east of Arabia might be a varied and complicated affair.

The primary task is to map some of this cultural variety and peg out the major chronological guidelines through the millennia in terms of

Fig 4. Wadi al Qawr, Ras al Khaimah: in the foreground a ruined settlement and beyond it the debris of mining.

the sites and monuments on the ground. The purpose of the field project in the Wadi al Qawr is to explore by survey and limited excavation the settlement history of a valley system ('wadi' is the Arabic word for valley) between the third millennium B.C. and the Islamic period. The Wadi al Qawr runs east out of the mountain range which points north to the Straits of Hormuz. At the simple level the survey is helping to fill out the picture of cultural variety up and down the Arabian peninsula. At a more complex level the objective of the work is to map and the ebb and flow of history within a particular area over a long period. At a local level, but of general significance, there is a third objective, to explore the way the settlement pattern changes as the wadi system is followed back from the Gulf coast and the coastal plain, through the foothills and deep into the mountainous hinterland. In particular, it is hoped to measure something of the depth of the impact of external inputs from the distant but powerful Mesopotamian and Indus Valley civilizations, as well as the cultural influences reaching across the Gulf from Iran at various periods. The gauge of the importance of external input to the local cultures is the penetration of imports from outside areas, recognisable as exotic articles in the local cultural context.

In the Wadi al Qawr, despite what may appear to our eyes to be a quite forbidding landscape, there are many sites, both settlements and cemeteries, of different periods. There are also areas of the valley where copper mining has been conducted. The work is still at an early stage, and only a few sites have been tested by excavation. Several tombs have been excavated to obtain a closer control on chronology through the medium of the many objects found in the graves. The comprehensive collection of artefacts also helps to broaden our appreciation of the cultural achievements of the people, especially in the widespread and long-lived industry in decorated bowls of soft stone.

Small-scale excavation has begun on a settlement of the first millennium B.C. about 35 km up the valley from the Indian Ocean coast. The finds are shedding light on the cleverly adapted mixed farming economy which supported the community, and on the extensive cultural links with far away places via the Indian Ocean seaways. Extensive copper mining activity has been dated to the 9th century A.D. and that, together with the find of a coin hoard of that period, suggests that the wadi and its mining industry was part of the hinterland of Sohar, one of the most famous Arabian ports of the period.

Reconstructing an ancient environment: Eskmeals, Cumbria

Over recent years we have seen an increasing general awareness of the importance of ecological ideas, which set man's activities as a factor in the shaping of the environment and at the same time show how intimately environmental factors impinge on human concerns. Perhaps archaeologists have played some part in sharpening the this appreciationof the importance of the relationship between man and environment. Certainly, because of their concern with simpler societies which were much more directly dependent on the resources of their physical environment, archaeologists have long sought the means to reconstruct the nature of the physical environment within which the people that they aim to study lived and obtained their livelihoods.

Environmental archaeology is now an important and highly inter-disciplinary aspect of the discipline of archaeology. Many sources of information may be tapped, ranging from the overall shaping of the landscape (geomorphology), through the processes of soil formation, to the recovery of traces of the original flora and fauna, includingthe identification of fauna such as beetles or snails, and the counting of microscopic pollen grains, and the physical and chemical analysis of amorphous residues.

In any project several of these sources of information may be applicable, and each requires a specialist skill in its investigation. Together with the group of archaeological specialists, therefore, there may be working several specialists in palaeoenvironmental analysis. A good deal of the data relating to the environment will also bear on the use of the resources in that environment by the community under archaeological investigation. For example, the animal bones recovered in excavation may be the only direct evidence of the fauna which lived in the landscape; but the bones are also the waste product of the butchery which filled the cooking pot with meat. If a useful synthesis of all this information is to be achieved, the task is one of close interdisciplinary cooperation between a number of specialists.

A good example of the process of synthesis which brings together the archaeologists and the environmental scientists is the Eskmeals project, in which the lives of hunter-gatherer groups who inhabited the Cumbrian coast some five to seven thousand years ago is being investigated. The archaeology of the habitation sites of these hunter-gatherers is described in the next section. Here we look at the attempt to discover something of the landscape which they found — rather different from today's — and to understand why these groups kept returning to this particular area, how they were able to establish fairly long-term encampments, and what were the resources which they exploited as their food supply.

Although the dense scatters of flint which mark the sites of the ancient encampments are now up to a kilometre from the present shoreline, detailed geological and geomorphological mapping has shown that the artefact concentrations lie strung along the line of an old, low cliff-line. Beyond the now scarcely perceptible cliff is a complex pattern of coastal and estuarine sediments. As well as the interface between land and sea, there is the additional factor of the estuaries of several small rivers to complicate the picture. Shingle ridges, wind-blown sand sheets, sand dunes and muddy silts show where there were formerly coastlines, salt marshes and stream courses.

The shingle ridges closest to the old cliff are several metres above the present sea-level, implying that they were deposited at a time of higher sea-level. Changes in sea-level have been complex over the millennia since the last glacial maximum. As the massive glaciers melted and the huge weight of ice was dissipated, the land-mass rose; in general the melting of the glaciers tended to increase sea-levels, but the inter-relation of rising land and changing sea-level brought about complicated oscillations of relative sea-level. The highest sea-levels around Britain were reached about 6 or 7 thousand years ago. Diatom analysis (see the section on this subject in the chapter about new directions in archaeology) on one of the excavated archaeological sites shows a change during the use of the site from marine to brackish water conditions. The implication is that the site was in use at the time when sea-level was beginning to drop, and the lagoon below the low cliff was becoming an estuary. The radiocarbon dates from the site confirm that it was indeed in use close to the time of highest sea-level.

As the sea-level dropped successive shingle ridges formed and were left behind by further sea-level change. The depressions between the shingle ridges were infilled with muddy sediments. Diatom analysis tells us that these sediments were also estuarine in character. The archaeologists suspected that the area had been chosen by hunter-gatherers because of the variety and richness of the ecological niche provided by the estuary. The absence of surface indications of frequent encampment further along the coast, where it is an open sea-shore, seemed suggestive.

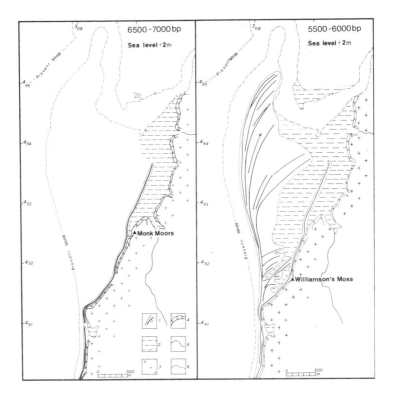

Fig 5.   As the foreland at Eskmeals changed through time, the settlements moved down the coast.

So it was important to establish the date of the encampments relative to the changes of sea-level and estuarine sediments. At one extreme the period was defined by the sea-level maximum, and at the other it was terminated by the completion of the infilling of estuarine sediments. Two of the dense concentrations of flint have been excavated to reveal the remains of encampments dated by radiocarbon to the early 7th millennium and the mid 6th millennium B.C. The earlier site, as has been mentioned, was dated to the time

33

when the marine water nearby was changing to brackish water, that is, at the beginning of the period when the rich estuarine econiche had just formed. The later site was shown, again on diatom analysis, to have been adjacent to a sizeable body of fresh water, a former lake (now a peat bog). It appears that, over many centuries, hunter-gatherers shifted their encampment sites southwards as the estuary formed, changed, and silted up.

While the estuary may have formed the focus of attraction for the bands of hunter-gatherers, it is certain that they would also have used the resources of the hinterland. Our understanding of the vegetation of the region inland of the archaeological sites comes from pollen analysis from several peatbog sites. The dominant vegetation type of the coastal plain was a mixed deciduous woodland of oak and elm, with an understorey of hazel, at least in places. Around the lake margins alder, birch and willow grew in dense communities. The open landscape of today is quite different, but a trace of the survival of the lake margin woodlands is to be inferred from the placename element 'carr', which once denoted such wet woods.

Areas of open grassland began to appear only about 5500 years ago, and it is probable that the changes in the landscape were effected by man. One of these cleared areas was close to the freshwater lake referred to above, and its clearance coincides in date with the period of the encampment near by. The forest clearance was only an episode, however, and the forest began to regenerate after about 200 years, and the hunter-gatherers moved away.

Two observations in the vegetation record relate to this episode of open grassland. While tree pollen in general is reduced in favour of grasses and other light-loving plants of open ground, elm pollen in particular shows a dramatic decline. And parallel to the elm decline the pollen record shows the occurrence of an inconspicuous small herb, the ribwort plantain. Evidence of a significant 'elm decline' has been noted in many parts of Europe, and it has often been suggested that its coincidence with the appearance of the first farmers indicates their use of elm foliage as a winter feed for their livestock, a traditional practice still in evidence in some parts of Europe. Ribwort plantain is often accepted as indicating the presence of grazing herds. Together, the decline in one species and the occurrence of the other perhaps indicate that the hunter-gatherer population had begun to shift to pastoralism.

Section 2: Focus on Settlement

In this section we shall be looking at the question of how we can find out about the lives of people in the past. A lot of what we do is done in the towns, cities or villages where we live. Of course people are engaged in important activities away from settlements, whether agriculture, quarrying or mining, golf or whatever else, but the greatest concentration of activities and the greatest variety of activities will be represented in the settlement where we live and where most of us work – and the golfer will keep his clubs at home anyway. The archaeologist's means of investigating settlements is excavation, a practical activity whereby they most often come into the public eye. But the practical aspect of a motley group digging and scraping away in the dirt can easily obscure what is really going on.

Archaeologists excavate all sorts of sites, but in this section it is convenient to link excavation with settlement. There are some important points to make about excavation which will help to explain why archaeologists dig as they do. Excavation is a process of carefully observing and recording the taking apart of a site, and in that sense it is totally destructive; any part of a site which has been dug can never be dug again, so any failure to observe a point is information lost, and any point misunderstood will probably always mislead. Inevitably, excavation encounters the last stage first, and gets to the original state of the site at the end; in trying to reconstruct what happened on a site, the excavator has to contend with getting his information in reverse chronological order, the consequence before the cause.

Always the evidence which remains on a site is incomplete. Many things will never have been left behind, while others were made of materials which will not have survived in the soil. And a good deal depends on where the archaeologists choose to dig. Unless the excavators can excavate the whole site, which is often simply a physical and practical impossibility, they must select what part of the site they will dig, and necessarily that choice has to be made before they know enough to make an informed decision. If the site is uniform all over, of course it will not matter at all how much one digs or where; but what settlement do you know which is the same all through? Generally, the larger the settlement the more variable it is (compare the complexity of a large city with the relative simplicity of a small village), and at the same time the larger the settlement, the less of it can be dug, and the greater the chance of having an unrepresentative sample. So excavation is very much like detective work, requiring a balance between flair, imagination, and luck on the one hand and patient, scientific observation and meticulous recording on the other. In the end the excavator hopes to be able to reconstruct as much as possible of the history of the site, and to reconstruct what the people who created the site made and did there.

Where the excavation is taking place in a historical context, as for example in the centre of the City of London, it will be possible to relate the stratified structural history of the buildinglevels encountered directly to the known history of London and England. It may well be possible to recognise the physical effects of such clearly dateable events as the Great Fire of London in 1666, or to link certain buildings to the reigns of particular kings and queens through the evidence of coins found in tell-tale contexts. Where the historical context of the site is indistinct, or where the site was occupied in prehistoric times, it may be much less easy to reconstruct the history of the site. Often this can be done only in terms of the structural history of the site itself: the excavator will identify a sequence of building and re-building phases, whose only real significance may be in providing a chronological framework of some kind for the history of the settlement.

Excavating an archaeological site has been variously compared to taking apart a layer cake, and peeling successive skins off an onion. If the former simile betrays a taste for archaeological self-gratification, the latter hints at the tears of distress. Excavation can indeed be very rewarding, and even exciting; but reconstruction of a settlement and, more importantly, reconstruction of the life of those who lived there, can be a trying task. The fundamental pre-requisites are to have a chronological framework for the story of the site, and to reconstruct the physical structure of the settlement as the stage on which any drama is to be re-enacted and understood. The question always is how much further can one get beyond these fundamentals.

In terms of the everyday life of the settlement the archaeologist must contend with the facts that the excavation of the site may need to be less than complete, that the artifacts recovered will be only a fraction of what was once there, and that the contexts within which finds are made may not be a true guide to their original locations and relationships. The first two of those considerations mean that any reconstruction will necessarily be partial; we may know about only one part of a large settlement, or only about certain aspects of activity and life on the site. The third consideration is an important one when we begin to recognise that many of the artifacts found will have been discarded because they were worn out or broken, and that things do not necessarily remain exactly where they were last used once a site is finally abandoned. We have to face up to the fact that much of the remains recovered in an excavation were treated as rubbish by those who lived in the settlement, and that anything still serviceable when the house under excavation went out of use would probably have been removed.

Hence it is understandable that archaeologists are not being ghoulish when they become highly excited if they come across the scene of a disaster, such as the sudden entombment of the whole of the Roman city of Pompeii by volcanic dust many metres thick. In a fire or an earthquake, at the onset of an invading army, when a building collapses without warning, many things get left just where they were as people flee or are themselves trapped, and for once we have the opportunity to observe things as if caught in a photograph.

For a long time it was thought that life in the remote prehistoric past had been a peaceful idyll lived in utopian circumstances of self-sufficiency, absence of competition and primitive democratic equality. The hillforts which conspicuously crown so many of the hill-tops of Britain and northwest Europe were explained as the hasty and anxious response of the Celtic tribes to the threat of Roman invasion. Now we know that many hillforts were first fortified several hundred years B.C., that they had a long history of periodic rebuilding and re-modelling, but that the fortifications had in many cases finally been abandoned and left to decay long before Roman times.

In recent years more and more evidence has been coming to light of warfare and conflict in much earlier periods. What were once thought to be simple enclosures of the English Neolithic period of about 3000 BC are now shown to have been defended settlements. The early use of metals throughout Europe and the Near East was extensively for the manufacture of weapons, whether for actual use in battle or more generally for display and the emphasis of superior warrior status. Defensive arrangements around settlements tend to be fairly readily found, and when the life of the settlement was brought to an abrupt end by enemy attack the archaeologist may be fortunate enough to stumble into one of those photographic stills where people and things were trapped in disaster, collapse or conflagration in ways which we rarely otherwise see.

When a settlement is excavated the archaeologists will of course want to know more than just the architectural form of the buildings and the mundane details of the daily lives of the people who lived in them. The construction and maintenance of defences around the settlement are fairly obvious indications of the level of social and political organisation within the community, as well as the broader canvas of relations between communities. Other indicators of the social and political conditions may be found, as also more sophisticated clues on the economic fabric of the life of the community. Much of the evidence will be discerned not just in terms of the structures and the strata, but in terms of the contexts of finds of all kinds and all sizes, and the search for patterns in the remains.

In reality there is no simple dividing line between the process of excavation and the process of analysis of the findings of an excavation. Two of the prime objectives of an excavation plan will therefore be to ensure the optimum conditions for the observation of the vitally important relations between structures, stratified deposits, artefacts and other small remains of all kinds; and to seek to analyse what is being found as it is found in order that the information can be fed back into the excavation. In consequence excavations tend to look rather leisurely affairs, while the diggers may seem to be obsessively concerned with tidiness. On the one hand what is being found must be carefully observed and meticulously recorded, while the team must also ensure that proper communication is maintained up and down the carefully defined lines of command and control from the kneeling troweller to the perambulating director. On the other hand the archaeologists will be constantly modifying their ideas and changing the questions which they ask of the site as their perception and understanding of it change under the influence of their discoveries day by day. Even so, on most excavations it is impossible to keep fully abreast of the implications of all that is being found as it is found, and post-excavation re-analysis of the records, the drawings, the photographs, the bones, the charcoal, the pottery and much else usually leads to changes of idea and even to new insights. Further illustrations of how we can learn about the economies, social or political organisation, even the ideologies and religious beliefs of extinct societies are offered in the following chapters.

Eskmeals, Cumbria, England

A group of sites dating back more than five thousand years has been the subject of investigation at the mouth of the river Esk on the coast of Cumbria in N.W. England. The sites represent the periodic use of the area over a period of more than a thousand years by hunter-gatherer groups, and the purpose of the multi-disciplinary project is to investigate the relationship between the human groups and the environment, which was a rather special and constantly changing one. A good deal of the work has been put into the recovery of information about the nature of the locality and the potential food resources it offered at the remote period of its use. The intricate task of reconstructing the changing sea-levels, the development of shingle banks, the estuarine sedimentation of the channels among the banks, and the vegetation of the landward hinterland have been described at the end of the previous section. Here we can concentrate on the information coming from the sites of the encampments themselves.

One of the discoveries of recent years, not only in Britain, but also in various other European countries as well as in the Near East, has been that hunter-gatherer life-style began to change in a very important way after the end of the geological Pleistocene Period, or Ice Age. It had long been known that there was a change in the pattern of hunting as the large herd animals which had supplied so much of he basic diet in earlier times (for example, reindeer, wild cattle, bison, and wild horse) either became extinct or at least became much rarer. In post-glacial times many hunter-gatherers developed new economic strategies in which they combined resources from a variety of different and complementary environmental zones. Places where contrasting environments met offered opportunities for longer term settlement. Thus the exploitation of the resources of the sea, the sea-shore, the estuary, the river and the landward area seems to have supported a group who spent a good deal of their time at Eskmeals.

The locations of hunter-gatherer encampments have been recovered because of the dense scatters of chipped flint occurring on the surface. Two of the sites were selected for excavation, and here we concentrate on the site at Williamson's Moss, which is still under excavation. The site, which has been radiocarbon dated to about 5500 years ago, was located on the edge of slightly higher ground (in fact, the low cliff of a former shore-line), looking out across the estuary of the River Esk, and close beside a small stream.

Where the flint scatter had been densest on the higher ground there was little sign of settlement. But the site was found to continue down towards the bank of the little stream, now long silted up and buried. In part because this part of the site was so well buried, it had been very little disturbed by modern ploughing or by roots or burrowing animals. Down by the buried stream-bed soil conditions were waterlogged and the archaeologists were delighted when they began to find well-preserved pieces of timber and birch bark.

As the painstakingly detailed excavations have continued they have revealed several areas in which birch bark flooring had been laid, and areas where platforms had been built on the soft edges of the stream, and indeed out into the stream bed. The platforms were constructed either of a lattice of large branches or parts of tree trunks laid criss-cross as the basis for a brushwood upper level, or as made ground, that is a mixture of stones, clay and soil dumped between horizontal retaining timbers. While the bigger timbers, large portions of oak tree trunks, show no signs of having been felled and were therefore probably retrieved as driftwood from the estuary, a number of the pieces of wood exhibit clearly the marks of woodworking.

Some of the exposed structures seem likely to be parts of trackways, while others resemble platforms, on which other structures may have been built. At present, with only relatively small areas excavated of what is apparently a very extensive area of timber construction, it is too early to attempt to reconstruct how the evidence should be fitted together. Were the trackways to facilitate egress out to the estuarine areas? Were the platforms constructed for assisting with the netting, spearing or trapping of salmon or sea trout, which are known to come in great numbers to spawn in the mouths of small channels and feeder streams leading off the present estuary?

If the site preserves timber, brushwood and bark, there is a good chance that other organic residues will be recovered to indicate what food resources were being exploited, and even at what seasons of the year. The potential resources of the coast, the estuary and the landward hinterland may well have been enough in combination to support year-round occupation at Williamson's Moss. Certainly the investment of effort involved in the construction of the extensive platforms and trackways suggests that the community which used this site were there for considerable periods. From the pollen evidence they would also seem to have been responsible for causing important changes in the landscape, removing trees and opening up areas of grassland.

The future research on this site will be aimed at discovering if this late hunter-gatherer community was in the process of becoming fully sedentary, that is year-round inhabitants of a permanent settlement, and how they supported themselves from the available food resources in the adjacent territory.

Mosphilia, Southwest Cyprus.

The excavation of part of the settlement at Mosphilia in the south-west of Cyprus is one aspect of a research project which combines survey and excavation. Mosphilia itself dates to about 4500-2500 B.C. and represents a series of stages in the cultural and social evolution of Cyprus' island population. As with the investigation of many of the other sites of earlier prehistoric times, the team working at Mosphilia is interested in producing evidence bearing on different levels of the life of the community.

It was once orthodox archaeological belief that until the coming of the first urban communities, and with them the early civilizations such as those of Egypt and Mesopotamia, village- farming life was simple and basically self-sufficient. In fact, what archaeologists have been learning for some years now is that social conditions in these early periods before the beginnings of urban civilization were far from egalitarian, tensions were considerable, and the economy was already much more sophisticated than the simple model of small communities of self-sufficient farmers suggests.

Mosphilia demonstrates these social, political and economic sophistications. The complexly stratified building remains testify to a quite lengthy history of occupation. The buildings were circular in plan, and enough survives to make possible their general reconstruction on paper. The largest buildings all belong to the third of the five phases of the settlement's history. In addition to their scale these houses are also more carefully constructed and their size and sophistication of construction is reinforced by the high quality of the artefacts found in them.

One of the buildings met its end in a fire, which is a particular piece of good fortune for the archaeologists. Embedded in the ash of the fallen and burnt roof members was found a remarkable concentration not only of the everyday storage pots but also the standard-sized bowls which served as measuring ladles. Analysis of the context of artefacts and organic remains is crucial to the unravelling of their functions within the living household. Altogether forty large storage pots have been restored from the thousands of crushed fragments.

Fig 6.   The large huse at Mosphilia under excavation. The remains of the collapsed roof have been removed to reveal the great array of crushed storage vessels.

However, there were only stone settings for eleven roundbased storage vessels; and the number of pots recovered were more than enough to cover the whole floor of the house. So the archaeologists can infer the presence of a loft or a stacked arrangement of pots.

This particular building at Mosphilia was larger than the other houses in the settlement at that period. It possessed a disproportionate amount of stored goods considerable. The volume of potehtial storage seems much greater than a single family could require for their own consumption, so it would seem that a minority at Mosphilia were exerting control through the concentration and control of economic resources.

Size and quantity of goods are not the only ways in which 'wealth centres' have been distinguished at Mosphilia. After the destruction of the house with the concentration of storage pots, another smaller one was placed inside and above its ruins. This building contained evidence for working flint, making beads from the marine shell dentalium, rare shell amulets and possibly the working of the metal copper. From the same house came the earliest sealstone yet found in Cyprus. In the neighbouring lands of S. W. Asia similar seals were used to identify property and to provide authorised documentation on goods which were stored or transmitted from place to place. It is easy to think that the seal performed the same function in Cyprus, found as it was in the context of what would appear to be an organised centre of manufacture. There is some evidence to suggest that the seal-stone had originated in the earlier storehouse, where its use to stamp identifications on the sealings of the storage-pots would make even greater sense. Though there is no evidence for highly specialised economy and a complexly organised society at this stage in Cyprus, it is clear that the beginnings of the process of development of bureaucratic control of economic activity and wealth were to hand.

Newmill, Perthshire, Scotland.

Newmill is a farm on the main road which leads north from Perth into the Scottish Highlands. The excavation of the ancient site was necessarily an emergency job to salvage as much information as possible within a very tight timetable. An area of a few hundred square metres in the middle of some road works was all that could be dug, but that area included the key parts of the original settlement.

The site fell into two quite different parts, one stone-built and below ground level, the other at ground level and originally timber built. The long, curving, stone-built structure was of a well-known type, which local people have called 'earthhouses' and archaeologists refer to as 'souterrains' (which is simply the French word for any underground chamber). Although souterrains have been turning up by accident in the East of Scotland (and elsewhere in North- west Europe) for at least two hundred years, little was known of their purpose or even their age. The opportunity offered by the chance discovery at Newmill was therefore to try to recover dating information, especially in the form of charcoal for radiocarbon dating, to look again for evidence of the function of a souterrain using contemporary excavation methods and to see if it was possible to relate a souterrain to what existed above ground at the same date.

There were hardly any artefacts on the site, and therefore no chance of using pottery or any other such dateable material. The radiocarbon dating samples of charcoal were vital, and showed that the settlement had been in use at least as early as the first century B.C., throughout the time when Rome's legions had shown a periodic interest in annexing Scotland into the Empire, and onwards until some time late in the first millennium A.D., when that part of Scotland was a Christian kingdom of the early medieval period.

The souterrain itself provided very little information about its function. It consisted of huge, blank, dry-stone walls up to two metres tall and a payed floor. There was no trace of the roof, but it may be guessed that it was timber-framed, since the width of the chamber (up to 4 metres) was too great for spanning with stone slabs, as can still be seen at some surviving souterrains. There were two doorways close together at one end, but no internal features and no finds on the floor. The popular idea of the souterrain as an underground dwelling seemed improbable because of the lack of a fireplace and any signs of

Fig 7. Reconstruction drawing of the large timber house with its souterrain at Newmill in Perthshire.

domestic use. In fact the souterrain had been kept remarkably clean; whatever its use was, it meant that even the cracks between the stones of the floor were meticulously kept free of dust or soil.

The other part of the site at ground level above the souterrain was quite different. There were found many cylindrical holes of all sorts of different sizes cut into the gravel subsoil. When they were excavated it was possible to see that they had once held timber uprights. The wood had of course decayed, but the stones which had been packed around the bases of the posts often retained a negative impression of the vanished wood. There were so many postholes that it was clear that they could not all belong to one building; presumably timber-framed buildings had been built one after another on the same site. It was like a 'join-the-dots' puzzle with the added ingredients that the dots were not numbered, and there were several sets of dots super-imposed on one another.

Only one building in the end could be fully disentangled, and that, as it happened, was the last in the series. The key feature of this house was a ring of eleven massive posts each about 20 cm in diameter and with more than one metre of its length buried in its post-hole. Such posts were clearly very tall and required to carry considerable structural forces. Knowing the centre of the circle it was then possible to identify an outer ring of much smaller posts which represented the line of the outer wall of the building.

An excavated house of very similar size and plan had been made the basis for a reconstruction experiment at the Butser experimental Iron Age farm in Sussex. The house at Newmill can be reconstructed using the Butser experimental rebuilding to show that the point of its roof would have stood more than 10 metres tall (a modern two-storey house is about 6 or 7 metres high). The thatched roof of the Butser house weighed about 45 tons, which explains why the ring of main structural posts were so large and so well-founded. The floor area of the Newmill house would have been about 243 square metres or more than 2500 square feet (a typical modern family house in Britain would be less than half that area).

Radiocarbon dates from the postholes of this latest house and from the construction phase of the souterrain showed that they were built about the same time. Perhaps the function of the souterrain could be understood in terms of the relationship between the souterrain and the contemporary timber house which stood beside it. In fact, as the plan of the house began to become clear it was found that its outer wall curved across the head of the main door of the souterrain.

The obvious reconstruction is that the souterrain functioned as a cellar to the people who lived in the timber house. A dry- stone construction set into free-draining gravel would remain cool, dry and even in temperature, as other surviving, stone- roofed souterrains demonstrate, and would provide good storage conditions for grain and other dry food products. While we are used to cellars which are constructed below the house, the Newmill solution was to keep their traditional earth floor and to build an external cellar. A nice refinement was to provide access to the souterrain from within the house, presumably so that goods could be extracted from the souterrain for use in the house, while the second doorway allowed goods to be put into the souterrain without the need to go through the house.

The great, circular house beside the souterrain would have been the largest in the settlement almost without doubt, because it one of the biggest ever to have been discovered in Britain. In that context it is of consequence that the storage capacity of the souterrain would have been enough to feed a whole village, and was much greater than needed simply for the feeding of the household to which the souterrain was attached. What the evidence seems to suggest is that the Newmill settlement was focussed on one household who were superior to the rest of the community, and whose role in the social and political fabric of the times was to concentrate and control of large volumes of the basic form of economic wealth, agricultural produce.

Inveresk, Mid Lothian, Scotland.

Inveresk lies East of Edinburgh on the southern side of the Firth of Forth. When the Roman army was intent on incorporating Scotland, or at least a sizeable part of it, into the Roman Empire, a major linear defence was built across Scotland from the Firth of Forth to the Firth of Clyde. For a while this defence, known as the Antonine Wall, replaced Hadrian's Wall, which lies further south, stretching from Newcastle to Carlisle. Beyond the eastern and western ends of the Antonine Wall itself were additional forts to guard the flanks. One of these forts is known to exist under the medieval and modern village of Inveresk, and outside the strict confines of the fort itself lies a settlement of the type which the Romans called a vicus.

Most of the vicus lies below modern houses, roads and gardens, but a part which had not been built over was excavated recently. The occasion of the excavation was once again a rescue task. Only a small part of the vicus was available, but nevertheless the excavations allowed the archaeologists to answer some important and fundamental questions about what kind of settlement a vicus was.

Some historians had speculated that the vicus settlement might be where local inhabitants had moved in order to provide for army requirements either in terms of supplies, or civilian labour, or in terms of servicing the soldiers' leisure requirements with taverns and the like. In the vicus, it was said by some, native Britons might acquire a knowledge of and a taste for the Roman way of life. And in this way the vicus settlements would perhaps have exerted an important, if informal, role in the primary Romanisation of natives in the military, front-line zone of the new province.

The question for the archaeologist was how to discern who lived in the vicus, and what was their cultural and economic relationship with the Roman garrison in the fort to which the vicus had attached itself. There was nothing to indicate the presence of a local native Iron Age population. The occupants of the annexe used pottery and other things which originated in the south of Britain or in Roman Gaul, and it is probable that these longdistance links reflect the main supply routes of the Roman army in Scotland.

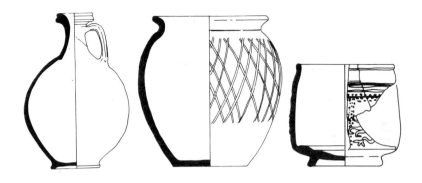

Fig 8. Romano-British pottery of southern British types, but made from local clays: Inveresk, Mid Lothian.

There was also a locally produced type of pottery, called now 'Inveresk ware' after the site where it was first identified. Although Inveresk ware closely resembles particular types of pottery known to have been manufactured in kilns in the south of England, neutron activation analysis of the fabric has shown that it was in fact made of a very different clay. It would appear that this simple-seeming pottery is an indication of the presence at Inveresk of craftsmen from the Romanised south of the province who had moved to the new settlement in order to set up local manufactures in response to the market opportunity which the supply of the frontier forces offered.

The nature of the contact between the Roman military or their civilian suppliers and the native Iron Age population remains highly problematical. We know that some Roman pottery, a few coins, and the odd small glass vessel found their way to native sites. At all events it would seem that the native peoples maintained their separate identity in the face of the Roman military presence and the very strong cultural influences which it brought with it. It is going to be rather difficult to assess the degree of contact in these circumstances; and yet it is difficult to imagine that absolutely all the Roman quartermaster's supplies were imported, and that none of the staples of the soldiers' diet was obtained from local farming communities.

Prehistoric settlement in the Outer Hebrides

Compared to the Northern Isles and other regions of mainland Britain the archaeology of the Outer Hebrides has attracted relatively little attention and fieldwork, although the Royal Commission on Ancient and Historical Monuments published its Inventory of the islands in 1928, drawing attention to the wealth of ancient and more recent monuments in the landscape. Since 1984 the Department of Archaeology at Edinburgh University has been endeavouring to remedy this neglect and to exploit the very rich potential of the Western Isles through a programme of air-survey, underwater survey and excavation.

Excavation has been focused at Loch Olabhat in North Uist and on the Miavaig peninsula of north-west Lewis, where the characteristic field monuments of the later prehistoric period include island brochs and duns, and wheelhouses located in the coastal machair lands. The current programme of investigation is concentrated on a widespread class of island settlements, revealing a remarkable span of occupation from neolithic to pre-Norse times, some three thousand years in all. By island settlement in this context is meant the use of an islet in a loch for the construction of a defensively designed homestead.

At Eilean Domhnuill in Loch Olabhat, North Uist, two seasons of excavation have been conducted at the time of writing on a site which is playing an important part in re-shaping our perceptions of the settlement history of Hebridean island occupation. The circular building on the little islet of Eilean Domhnuill had been classified, like hundreds of others, as a dun and assumed to date to the last centuries B.C. The excavation at once began to make it apparent that this site belonged some 2500 years or more earlier than the other excavated and dated duns. The dating evidence is quite explicit, taking the form of many thoroughly recognisable sherds of neolithic pottery of a style well known from dated neolithic chambered tombs in the Hebrides. The implication of this quite unexpected dating is that it will be necessary to reconsider the dating of all the other unexcavated sites which have been labelled as duns and assumed to belong the closing centuries of the first millennium B.C.

The small stone-walled house on Eilean Domhnuill was oval or subrectangular in plan, used a number of wooden posts in its structure (a point worth remarking since the site exists in what is now a virtually tree-less landscape). In the centre of the floor was constructed a hearth. Outside the house, around the periphery of the little island, midden deposits have been found, the lower parts of which are below the water table and are therefore waterlogged, preserving materials such as seeds, objects of wood, and large quantities of hazelnut shells. The potential of this midden material for shedding light on the neolithic economy and environment of the Hebrides is very considerable.

On an artificially reinforced outcrop which forms a small island in Loch Bharabhat the archaeologists are working on an Iron Age dun, an oval, stonebuilt, fortified farmstead. Access to the island was controlled by an artificial causeway, which linked it to the west shore of the loch. The objective of the investigation is to learn something of the economy and function of such isolated settlements; and that objective is greatly assisted by the combination of conventional excavation techniques with underwater excavation, because of the remarkable conditions of organic preservation which obtain in the still waters of the loch.

The dun measures about 10 metres by 11.5 metres. Its entrance was designed to be at the opposite side of the building from the access causeway, requiring any visitor to walk right round the building on a narrow catwalk below the wall. Everything is designed for security. The pivot stone which supported the sturdy wooden door is in place, and one can see how the doorway was constructed with a protective rebate against which the door could sit, and barholes in the stonework to house a strong wooden beam to close the door. In the thickness of the massive dry-stone wall were three intramural galleries, one of which led to a flight of steps providing access to an upper floor or to the wall-head.

The small finds indicate that the life of the dun was fairly short, from the closing centuries B.C. into the 1st century A.D. In its last phase of use, which was after the dun structure had at least partly collapsed, the ruins were re-used for some industrial activity such as bronze-working which required furnaces and hearths.

An important aspect of the Bharabhat excavations has been the investigation of the underwater deposits adjacent to the dun. In the shallow water margins on the east side of the island have been found several lengths of walling and the debris of occupation at a depth of up to a metre below the present level of the loch, and it is thought that these may relate to an earlier period of activity, before the dun was built. The implication is that the present loch level is the same as that which protected the island dun, but that the level may have been raised (artificially?) after the initial period of occupation and before the island dun was built.

The underwater excavations from around the margin of the island are producing quantities of bone, shell, and other organic materials such as wooden artefacts and heather-rope, which would not survive

Fig 9. Careful excavation of the post-broch re-occupation levels in the island broch at Loch na Berie, Lewis.

on any land-based site. Even straw, probably the litter from an Iron Age byre, survives under the water, still golden in colour when first exposed.

At the nearby Loch na Berie, which is now almost totally silted up, a longer sequence of occupation has been found. The original structure on the island in the loch was a circular, stone-built broch with an overall diameter of about 18 metres, which was approached from the west by a causeway. The little island was located on the edge of a coastal inlet, or possibly within a slack behind the accumulating dunes of the Traigh na Berie. Soil has accumulated in great quantities since the broch's abandonment, which means that the capstones which roof its galleries have survived in place at about the modern ground level. The archaeological deposits in these galleries, undisturbed and sealed in waterlogged conditions, will afford a wonderful opportunity to recover artefacts made of organic materials and important environmental evidence, once the excavation reaches them.

Several centuries after the broch had been abandoned to fall into ruins, probably in the early centuries A.D., the site was re-occupied in pre-Norse times. Around the 7th or 8th centuries A.D. a remarkable figure-of-eight shaped structure was built within the walls of the former broch. The method of construction, using vertical slabs set against the collapse debris of the broch, with horizontal dry-stone coursing above, is paralleled in buildings of the Pictish period elsewhere, but is so far unique in Lewis. This building had its doorway superimposed on the entrance to the earlier broch. In the centre of the interior was a hearth, and there was also a pair of niches, or 'seats' set into the west wall. Finds from this later phase of re-occupation include nearly two dozen bone pins, fragments of a bone comb, two small crucibles and a pair of bronze tweezers.

Work will continue on the Berie site, and may be expected to yield further phases of occupation intermediate between the pre-Norse, or Pictish, final phase and the primary broch occupation. The consequence of the slow rise in the surrounding ground level, which was caused by local changes in the coastal geomorphology, has been that successive periods of re- occupation are conveniently vertically separated, and have been even more conveniently sealed and preserved. Consequently the Berie site promises a long and richly detailed account of the changing patterns of life over a period of many centuries.

At other sites already located there are known to be lengthy occupation sequences underlying the Iron Age levels of the last phase of occupation. In sum, taking the evidence of a neolithic occupation at Eilean Domhnuill, the suggestion of long, pre-Iron Age occupations at some sites, and well-attested use of duns, brochs and later forms of round house from the later Iron Age to the dawn of the Norse period, it appears that the researchers may be beginning to grasp a huge continuum of settlement on the small island sites covering more than three thousand years.

Carn Brea, Cornwall, England

One of the aspects of life which the early sedentary societies share with communities of later times, indeed up to our own times, is the prevalence of competition, warfare and the importance of organised defence. Earlier in this century it was thought that early farmers colonised a nearly empty landscape in Europe, in which there was virtually no competition. In this view of prehistoric times conflict, warfare and the need for defence began to arise only in much later prehistoric times, being specially characteristic of the early states, urban civilizations, and their immediate predecessors.

In fact, there were scattered clues that life was not so simple, peaceful and self-sufficient. In Britain, skeletons found in collective burials dating to the Neolithic period, around 3000 B.C., showed signs of violent death, but these could be explained as the victims of personal quarrels, accidents or misadventures.

Carn Brea is a prominent hill-top site near Redruth in Cornwall. The site had been known since the 19th century for its visible remains of ramparts and the surface finds of objects of Neolithic age. Excavation in the early 1970's showed that the site was a strongly fortified permanent settlement, not just a fortified hill-top refuge. And the excavations also revealed unexpected evidence that the fortifications were not a needless precaution: the fortified township had been the scene of a desperate final battle which had ended in its disastrous overthrow and destruction.

The rampart around the summit of the hill was stone-built and massive, about 2 metres thick and 2.5 metres tall, and the careful taking apart of the mass of stonework showed that the collapse was sudden, complete and Neolithic in date. The defensive system had been more thorough and complex, however. Beyond the stone-built rampart around the summit were outer enclosures formed of stone-faced ramparts and sometimes accompanied by a flat-bottomed ditch cut into the rock. The intention was clearly defence in depth. The gateways of the enclosures were designed and constructed to give the defenders the advantage of flanking fire.

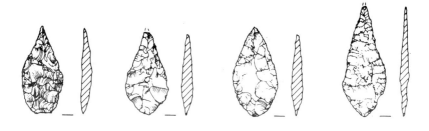

Fig 10. Leaf-shaped arrowheads were found in great numbers around the ramparts of Carn Brea; many of them had broken tips, as shown here.'

One type of artefact which had been commonly picked up by casual visitors to the site for centuries was a simple, leaf-shaped arrowhead of flint. Indeed, such leaf-shaped arrowheads are commonly found in the ploughsoil in certain parts of Britain, but they had been thought to be the tips of hunting arrows.

The excavation recovered more than 800 arrowheads, most of them broken, and many of them burnt in the final conflagration. The critical observation about the arrowheads was that they were almost all found around the inner rampart, both inside and outside where they had fallen; and no less than 150 arrowheads were thickly clustered at the gateway to the innermost enclosure. That this last attack ended in defeat for the Carn Brea residents is clear from the signs of burning, the destruction of the houses and the near total destruction of the great inner rampart.

Hambledon Hill, Dorset, England

Towering above the present-day village of Child Okeland in Dorset, in the very heart of Thomas Hardy country, is the great, rounded mass of Hambledon Hill, long known for its massive hill-fort of the last centuries before the Roman invasion. Beneath the clear traces of the hill-fort lie the much less clear remains of a neolithic complex.

In fact, Hambledon Hill in Neolithic times proved to be a good deal more complex than anyone had expected. There was a settlement of farmers living there in an enclosed and fortified village about one hectare in area; but beside that quite small enclosure there was another, far larger enclosure of about 9 hectares. The larger enclosure seems to have been a massive necropolis area where dead bodies were exposed to decay before they were buried. (More of the funerary practices uncovered at the site can be found in the section on the archaeology of society and belief.) Another facet of the complex is the existence of attendant long burial mounds; and the whole complex, settlement enclosure, necropolis enclosure, and burial mounds, was encompassed within a quite gigantic, multi-rampart defensive system which enclosed fully 60 hectares of land. The detailed evidence suggests that development of these defences was a gradual and complex process, which culminated in a double timberframed rampart with a further fence set beyond these two lines. As at Carn Brea, we seem to see an attempt to achieve defence in depth.

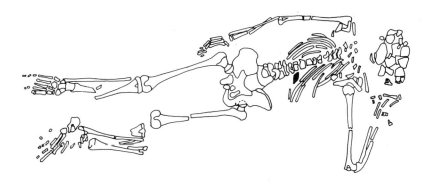

Fig 11.   Skeleton of a young man with a leaf-shaped arrowhead in his chest: Hambledon Hill, Dorset.

As at Carn Brea, however, the attempt appears to have been ultimately unsuccessful. On a day when a lively N. W. wind was blowing the timberfaced rampart was fired over a length of at least 150 metres on the S. face of the hill. The burning of the timber facing completely destabilised the whole rampart, and the mass of chalk rubble locked with the timber frame, much of it heavily scorched, poured forward into the ditch. Fortunately for the archaeologist, this collapse sealed the clearest evidence of the nature of the tragic events of that day.

Both the death and burial and the death in conflict aspects of Hambledon Hill's neolithic occupation are made much more vivid, since chalk is a very sympathetic subsoil for the preservation of bone. At Hambledon Hill we have the dramatic evidence of the well-preserved skeletal remains, which were missing in the soil conditions of Carn Brea. Beneath the rubble of the burnt timber and scorched chalk were found the skeletons of four young and robustly built adult males. One had a leafshaped arrowhead of flint embedded in his chest cavity, which had entered from his back. He had been apparently been shot fatally while carrying a tiny child, who was crushed by his forward fall into the ditch. With the evidence of the deployment of archery, the killing of a group of young men, the firing of the rampart and its destruction, it is inevitable that the conclusion is that warfare, however ritualised, is indicated.

Portknockie promontory fort, Banffshire, N. E. Scotland

The great number of hillforts in Britain and parts of northern and western Europe, together with the other fortified sites such as promontory forts, were usually interpreted as having been hurriedly erected in the face of the advancing legions of Rome, but it has emerged that these well-known monuments of the countryside are much more varied in date. Just as many fortified settlements are now known to date from much earlier than the Roman advance, so others have been shown to belong to the post-Roman Dark Ages.

Recent excavations at the Green Castle, Portknockie, have shown that this site's defensive constructions belong to a date well after the Roman period, in the very poorly known second half of the first millennium A.D. The rampart was built with an elaborate box-like framework of timbers, which it might be thought served to hold the rampart firmly together. However, as with other rampart designs, the Green Castle rampart seems to have been built with an eye directed more to appearance than to good structural and defensive principles.

The timber framework of the rampart is nowhere bedded into the ground; the horizontal members of the frame were simply laid on the ground surface. The inner wall-face of stone was curiously based on the top of the lowest timber member. And the outer wall-face was founded somewhat downslope; such a device would perhaps make the wall look more tall and impressive when seen from the outside, but the wall was rendered considerably less stable in consequence.

Levroux and Mont Beuvray, France.

In the last centuries B.C. hill-forts and various other kinds of defensive enclosure became common in many parts of northern and western Europe. In France and south-east England some of these enclosed settlements were very large indeed, encompassing tens or even hundreds of hectares. Julius Caesar in his account of his Gallic Wars refers to them as 'oppida', the Latin term for a sizeable town, and he also describes a particular type of fortification, which he termed the 'murus gallicus' (the Gallic wall-type). Julius Caesar described a stone-faced rampart construction with the beam-ends of the internal timber-lacing projecting and visible. In France in particular there was much use of iron spikes as long as 30 cm, which were augered into the crossing points of the timbers. Modern scholars have considered that the size of these oppida, the level of organization implied by the scale of their defences, and the industrial level of production which can be inferred from such evidence as the consumption of so much manufactured iron in the construction of ramparts contrive to suggest an initial phase of urbanisation in temperate Europe. This phase has been thought to date in the period immediately prior to Caesar's campaigns in the 1st century B.C., but detailed investigation is beginning to demand refinement of the former assumptions.

At Levroux, in the French Departement of Indre, joint excavations undertaken by the French archaeologists in cooperation with a British team have shown that the murus gallicus construction could not be so simply related to the historical event of the Roman military advance. In part the evidence for an earlier construction date consists of the dateable material accidentally incorporated with the construction material in the core of the murus gallicus rampart. But more important was the discovery that the stone- faced murus gallicus had been overlain with a massive dump rampart of limestone, which had been specially brought to the site from some distance. Such huge, sloping-fronted banks, often further reinforced by broad ditches, were already known from North-East France, where they seem to represent a response to the threats posed by Roman military technology (battering rams, catapults and sapping techniques).

Compared with the 20 hectares enclosed by Levroux's murus gallicus, the major oppidum of Bibracte (Mont Beuvray) in Burgundy is very large. The principal fortification (parts of whose outer line have only recently been identified in heavy woodland) runs for about 5.5 kilometres to enclose and area of approximately 135 hectàres. In certain sectors of the circuit the rampart plunges across the contours with scant regard for defensive considerations. Here, at the capital of the pro-Roman Aeduan tribe, is a classic example of a fortification where prestige, appearance and perhaps other factors which are more archaeologically elusive, such as the possible legal significance of the limits of the settlement, seem to have governed the form and line of the enclosure, while defensive considerations would appear to have been secondary considerations.

The recent excavations of the northern gate at Mont Beuvray are another example of Franco-British joint research. The scale of the entrance is truly impressive, with the gateway itself being recessed some 40 metres behind the perimeter line. The road approaches the gateway down a broad funnel some 20 metres wide. The long entrance passage, flanked by overweening ramparts, was embellished with other details which strongly suggest that its purpose was to impress new arrivals visiting the capital.

The combined results of the old and the new excavations suggest that five successive constructions and reconstructions of the massive defences were undertaken in rapid succession within the span of about a hundred years from the end of the second century B.C. Two of these constructions were classic muri gallici, although somewhat jerry-built. The last of the series was a simple dump bank of stone, very much the same pattern as has been found at a number of other sites.

Section 3: Sermons in Stones, and Clues in Every Thing

The theory of archaeology is that the things which we build, make and use and with which we surround ourselves are not only the tools which form the basic equipment of our lives (houses, clothes, pens, radios, cars etc) but are also a cultural code or language with which we communicate. The kind of house, the special clothes, our choice of ear-rings, that expensive red German car, even the piece of black plastic across its rear plus the letters 'GTi', everything we make and use, contains clues about who we are and how we relate to each other in the particular society in which we live. The same is true of other societies in other countries or at other times. The cultural language of their artefacts may be different, but the task of the archaeologist is to try to read that language in the cause of interpreting the history of past societies.

Archaeologists make a somewhat unreal distinction between the portable bits and pieces, which tend to end up in museum collections, and which archaeologists call artefacts, and the largescale artefacts which cannot be removed from their site, such as houses, stone circles or field boundaries, which usually stay where they were found, and which archaeologists do not usually think of as artefacts in the same sense. The distinction is a simply practical one viewed from the archaeologist's point of view and depends upon portability. A house, a grave or a cess-pit is as much an artefact (that is, fashioned by man's hand) as a drinking-cup or a jewelled brooch, and as much a potential source of information. In fact, there are many other things which an archaeologist may recover, which may have considerable latent information content, but which have not been fashioned or made by man, at least not in the simple and direct sense. The waste by-products of metal-working may be more informative about the technical processes employed in the workshop than the artifacts themselves which were the product. The animal bones which may inform us about diet, butchery fashions and farming practice, the charcoal in the ashes of the fireplace, which may tell us about the locally available tree species, the human remains in the grave, which represent the direct physical traces of the people themselves whose history we are intent on recovering, all these fossil traces of past human activity are as potentially informative as the products of human handicraft.

There are many ways in which we can use artefacts from the past as information sources. We can use artefacts as dating labels for particular periods. At the basic level we can find out what materials were in use, sometimes where and how they were obtained, and what were the techniques of manufacture employed. We can analyse the remains of foodstuffs and discover a good deal about animal husbandry, crops and food processing. In a variety of ways we can reconstruct the ordinary aspects of everyday life, though it may be quite difficult for us to reconstruct the practical functions of all sorts of tools which were once everyday household items. But what is particularly difficult to do is to read the deeper layers of significance in artefacts – why a particular weapon was made in precisely that form, or why a particular pattern was used as ornament.

A natural reaction of archaeologists when faced with a mass of artefacts from the past has been to classify them, to reduce the great formless heap into a series of smaller sets, each of which can be tackled sensibly and separately. In the early days of archaeology, when one of the most serious difficulties faced was that of seeking to inject some chronological perspective into prehistoric times, classification was seen as the first stage in representing time in terms of particular types of artefact. In examining, for example, the bronze tools and weapons of the European Bronze Age, the task would first be to identify a series of 'types', daggers as distinct from axes, swords as distinct from halberds, chisels as distinct from adzes, and so on. Each of these types could then be examined in order to discern internal variation. The archaeologist would then have to make some assumption about the dynamics of change through time within that type; one might assume that during the Bronze Age knowledge of the properties of metals and skills in handling them increased with time, and thus one might suggest that the technically simplest tools were the earliest, while the more efficient and effective designs, requiring a more complex technology in manufacture, came later. Having devised a succession of stages the archaeologist could then use artefacts to datestamp a burial or a settlement relative to a particular stage in the typological sequence. It should not sound far-fetched to us that such references to dating should be used, for we are quite accustomed to seeing the film-director or the maker of the period-drama for television establish the date of the story for us by clever visual references in the opening shots; we have only to see certain clues in the clothes worn, the jewellery or even the spectacles, or particular designs of motor-car in the street, and we quickly recognise the chronological setting.

But we can also recognise that artefacts are not only distinctive of time but also of place, or rather of different groups of people. For several generations now most of us in the Western world have been wearing practically identical clothes, so that it is no longer easy to distinguish an Italian man from a Frenchman, or a German, or an American in terms of his dress. However, we are all at least vaguely aware that the people of earlier generations wore highly distinctive folk costumes, especially on important social occasions. Such costumes enabled people to distinguish, often very precisely, where the wearers came from. Similarly visits to a series of folk-life museums in any country would enable one to recognise that the shape of tools, the design of horse-drawn wagons, the architecture of a barn or the way the straw was stacked might vary from area to area in (to our untutored eyes) subtle but no doubt thoroughly distinctive ways. This property of artefacts to be distinctive of the people of an area at a particular period has also been very useful to archaeologists as a means of labelling and mapping people who share certain cultural characteristics.

The real difficulty, of course, is in identifying what was the significance read in the artefacts by the people who made and used them, as distinct from what may appear to us distant observers to be distinctive or important. In our own cultural context we can recognise that artefacts can function simultaneously at different levels. The 'company car' serves to get the employee from place to place, but there is a distinct hierarchy of model and marque, which the manufacturers are very eager to encourage, whereby the humble sales representative may be very quickly distinguished from his area sales manager, and noone can mistake the company's senior executives. Only in certain branches of the Christian church will the ring worn by a bishop signify his role and command respect, but most of us will be familiar with the idea of 'respect for the cloth'. Once one begins to look around and analyse the extremely complex functioning of artefacts at all sorts of different levels in our own society, it soon becomes apparent that the reading of the symbolism or meaning in artefacts from cultural contexts removed from us in space and time must be a difficult and dangerous exercise.

Experiment

One of our present difficulties in interpreting the remains of the past is that we make so few of the artefacts we use and have so little direct experience of the properties of materials and the techniques of fabrication. Few of us could make a pot from clay, or build and thatch a wooden house, or make a knife or fork, let alone make any of those pieces of modern equipment (a television, a refrigerator or a micro-computer) which we consider essential parts of contemporary life and the typical products of our times. Considering that people used flint for hundreds of thousands of years for all their most important tools, it is all the more difficult for us to interpret and 'read' these stone tools, when nowadays chipped stone toolmaking is, for all but a very few of the people living in the world today, an entirely lost skill.

We can make up for some of these deficiencies through observation of people who still use the technologies we have forgotten. And we can experiment, trying to reconstruct methods of manufacture and techniques of use. We can also hope to learn something of the general functioning of artefacts at all levels within human cultures through experimental observation of attitudes to and use of artefacts among different cultural groups.

It is artificial to attempt to distinguish between experiment and controlled observation in the field. Often the experimenter will use as the starting-point already known information from some ethnographic or historical context. For example, very few of us today have actual experience of the use of bows and arrows in earnest, whether as weapons of war or as means of obtaining meat. If we found a group of flint arrowheads, could we tell if they were indicators of endemic warfare or the essential equipment of hunters? We can of course consult contemporary field archers, who will certainly know a great deal more than most of us about the nature of arrows. We can also consult historical documentation, whether in the form of written texts, pictures illustrating their use, or museum collections of surviving bows and arrows in order to learn about the functional characteristics of arrows meant for warfare. Or we might be able to see how contemporary serious practitioners of archery design their equipment for particular ends; especially if they are still using chipped stone for their arrowheads the information would be very valuable. And of course we may put the information together, make facsimile equipment as closely resembling the archaeological examples in which we are interested, and test it in controlled experimental conditions.

Both experiment and ethnographic observation are means of making up for the deficiencies in our present knowledge of the use of materials and artefacts. And their purpose is to enable us to make better and fuller use of the archaeological data in our hands.

Grimes Graves flint mines, Norfolk, England

With the appearance for the first time in Europe of economies based on farming we find flint mines from Poland to Belgium, from Sweden to Sicily, and in Britain from Sussex to Norfolk. Perhaps the denser population of stone-using people was enough to outstrip the capacity of surface-collected flint to serve the needs of the times. Other contributory factors may have been the new need for heavy edge-tools, such as axes, which would have been needed for land clearance and the preparation of timbers for house-building, fence construction and other activities.

The best known example of flint mines in Britain are those at Grimes Graves, near Brandon in Norfolk. When the opportunity arose some years ago to undertake a major new excavation at the site, the objective was to find out as much as possible of working practices of the miners and the economic basis of their activity. The task was to excavate one of the more than five hundred known shafts at the site (the surface over about 20 hectares is pocked with the hollows which mark refilled shafts and piled with spoil heaps). Radiocarbon dates assayed on picks made from red deer antler from earlier excavations had indicated that Grimes Graves was in use around 2000 B.C., several centuries later, as it happens than the dates obtained from mines in Sussex.

As to the way of life of the miners, there was precious little evidence around the shaft. Perhaps they lived at some distance from Grimes Graves on the fertile lands of the flood plain of the Little Ouse river some 2 km to the south. There were clues in the spoil heaps which they had thrown up from the workings as to the regime of working the mines. It appears that work was perhaps seasonal, with hundreds of tons of spoil being dumped in a long spell of working, followed by a pause, during which the surface of the dump began to weather. Maybe the miners were part-time farmers who needed to intermit their mining for tilling, planting and harvesting.

The shaft had been laboriously dug using only antler picks, antler rakes, and presumably baskets for carrying away the spoil. Care was taken to work the sides of the shaft so as to minimise the risk of lumps of chalk rubble falling away and dropping down the shaft at a later stage. Access was by means of ladders, which led down to a wooden staging erected at a height of about 2 metres above the floor of the

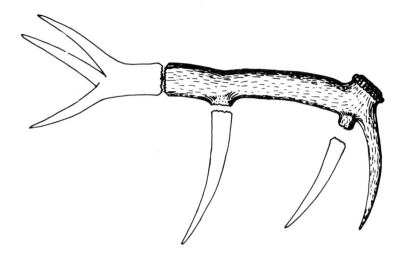

Fig 12. Picks made from the antlers of red deer were used to lever
out the chalk and flint lumps in the Grimes Graves flint
mines.

shaft. The staging, which was made of oak, was set precisely so that
the ascending ladder was at a convenient angle for the porters of
baskets of spoil; at the same time it provided overhead protection for
miners working at the base of the shaft. The whole operation was
clearly remarkably well organised, as evidenced by the profusion of
used and discarded red deer antler picks; what amounts to a
secondary industry must have existed to obtain and supply so many
antlers.

Reaching the level at which the seam of black tabular flint nodules
are found required a substantial initial investment, for the shaft had to
be taken down to a depth of about 13 metres, and more than 1000
tons of chalk rubble had to be dug, loaded in baskets, carried out and
dumped on the spoil heaps which surrounded the head of the shaft.
Once the flint seam was reached galleries were opened radiating
from the base of the shaft in every direction. The seam was followed
and exploited as extensively as was safe and economical. Illumination
was provided by oil lamps made from chalk lumps. Flint nodules were
levered out of the matrix of chalk and were then broken into rough
blocks for carrying to the surface. Minute examination of the floor of

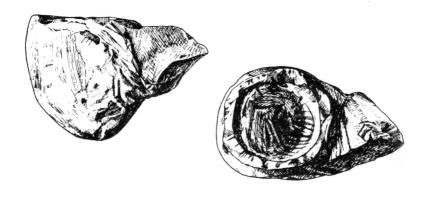

Fig 13. The only light in the galleries of the mine was supplied by small chalk lamps.

the shaft and galleries enabled the excavators to identify the find-spots of all the large nodules, which makes possible the estimation of the total yield of the mine. The very high quality flint from this one shaft (out of several hundred such shafts) would have been enough to produce 5000–10000 axes. Several million axes would have been produced over the several centuries of mining at Grimes Graves.

Once the broken down nodules had been got out of the shaft, they were taken to nearby working areas, where they were reduced by fairly coarse flaking to produce 'roughout' blanks of axes. Very few of the blanks were found at Grimes Graves, and the finishing of the product was carried out elsewhere. Finished products found their way to various parts of Britain, though by what means, whether by trade, or social gift exchange, we do not know. What is clear, however, is that the production of the flint was highly organised, very specialised and 'professional', and on a scale which we can recognise as industrial.

Functional analysis of chipped stone tools

Chipped stone tools have the archaeological advantage that they survive indefinitely; and, for the tens of thousands of years of man's early prehistory, chipped stone tools constituted the most important and the greater part of the tooikit. Very few people today, however, have direct experience of making or using stone tools. Archaeologists have always been interested in seeking to define how chipped stone tools were made and for what they were used, but their interpretation was for a long time based on analogies drawn from modern stone tool using peoples observed by anthropological field-researchers.

The founding father of the functional analysis of chipped stone tools has been the Soviet scholar Semenov, and now there are several groups of researchers working on different aspects of this approach to the study of stone tools. Under a low-powered microscope it becomes apparent that the use of chipped stone tools produces a variety of characteristic types of wear-mark. In some cases this wear amounts to quite conspicuous edge-damage, but at the other end of the spectrum there is an amazing range of polishes. One side of the research is concerned with the detection and characterisation of the various traces of wear and damage: the other side is the identification of the type of use which has produced the observed wear. This is done by means of experimental replication: stone tools are made from materials similar to those under study, and are then used in different ways on a variety of materials in order to produce a set of comparative scratches, polishes and scars under controlled conditions.

In many parts of the world, however, the locally available stone was a less than ideal raw material; and an important aspect of the development of functional analysis is the exploration of its application to types of stone with a coarser texture and poorer and less predictable flaking patterns than the classic, fine-grained flints. In looking at the cherts which were in use in the southern Scottish uplands, it has become apparent that the traces of use were not formed on that material as quickly or as clearly as is the case with flint. In addition there is an increased problem in dealing with the ease with which chert lost its working edge and quickly needed re-working. In all functional analysis there is also another source of difficulty in that chipped stone tools can easily acquire additional damage after they have been discarded.

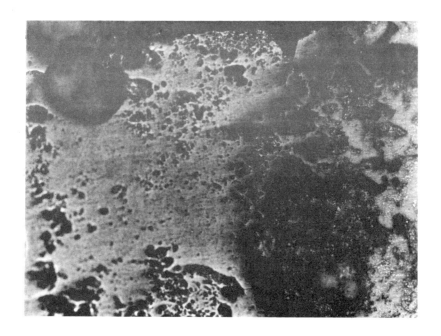

Fig 14.   Under the microscope the edge of this chert tool can be seen
to be polished with use.

Another aspect of the research is simply practical: it is necessary to ensure that the analysis is as efficiently conducted as possible in terms of results achieved for input of time and effort, and considerable attention is given to developing techniques which improve efficiency. Chipped stone assemblages often number thousands, or even tens of thousands, of pieces, and the speed at which the analysis can be conducted is obviously a crucial factor in its effectiveness.

As well as detecting the microscopic scratching or polishing, it is important to note the location of the wear-marks on the tool, the presence of any edge-damage, the relationship between the wear and the damage, and the gross shape and angle of the edge of the tool. In the parallel programme of experimental manufacture and replication of use it is possible to monitor precisely how the traces of

73

use develop, and what is possible (and impossible) with a tool of given shape. Further experiment has been conducted to see what damage is caused when abandoned chipped stone tools are trampled in the soil where they have been dropped.

Just as the average detective or forensic scientist can rarely equal the inductive precision of the fictional Sherlock Holmes, so it is usually too much to expect that the precise function of the individual tool can be ascribed to it by means of functional analysis. As a result of examining a large body of chipped stone tools the investigator can make more general statements about the culturally characteristic ways in which they were used. In any chipped stone tool industry, many of the pieces are in effect by-products of the process of manufacture, and were never intended as tools. The investigator will be able to say something about what proportion of the total chipped stone was in fact used as tools, how intensively tools were used, and whether they were used consistently for the one task. Some peoples are happy to use tools for any purpose as long as they work, while other cultural traditions prefer the 'right' tool for the job.

The analysed assemblage of chipped stone tools, along with other aspects of the remains, will also help to construct a picture of the range and type of activities which were pursued on a site. Some sites may have been specialised in purpose, while others were the scenes of very generalised activity. Within a settlement, as is the case in our own settlements, it may be that there is quite specific zoning of different aspects of life, and functional analysis of chipped stone tools can then help in the recognition of general domestic areas, places of tool manufacture, and workshop areas where the tools are employed for particular purposes.

Bronze Age weapons in the Near East

The investigation of the ways in which our ancestors learned to manipulate new materials, and how they then employed those materials to make things is not just a matter of uncovering the history of technical discovery and invention. A society's interest in technological experiment and innovation, and in particular the way in which a society chooses to incorporate a new material into its material culture can be very informative about social and cultural attitudes. Nowhere is this better illustrated than in the employment of copper and bronze in the period we call the Bronze Age in the countries of the Levant.

We now know that a knowledge of the properties of metals and skills in such metallurgical processes as alloying and casting were already well worked out long before the beginning of the so-called Bronze Age around 3000 B.C. Yet it is many centuries later when metal products begin to become relatively common in the archaeological record. When we do find evidence of the use of metals it is noticeable that many of the finds are weapons of war, and that our finds come mostly from tombs and to a lesser extent from deliberate deposits of groups of weapons buried in the ground.

It seems that the use of metals was strongly influenced by social and political factors, and also by economic factors: technical factors would appear to be relatively unimportant. The economic aspect of weapon production is reflected in the presence or absence of tin in the copper-based metal. There are no natural resources of tin in the Levant, and metal-smiths often used small quantities of arsenic to improve the casting characteristics of their copper. When they learned of tin by whatever means, supplies of this superior alloying agent had to be obtained from distant markets, and it remained relatively uncommon for several centuries.

The appearance of metal weapons in tombs coincides with a change in burial practice. At a time fairly late in the third millennium B.C. the practice of collective burial in a rock-cut burial chamber gave way to various forms of single burial. The single burials are often accompanied by grave-goods, which may include weapons with the male burials. It is tempting to think that the change in burial custom from collective to individual interment should be understood in parallel with the increase in quantity and quality of grave-goods: the

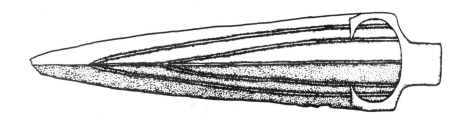

Fig 15. An elaborately cast veined dagger from a Levantine tomb dating to about 1800 B.C.

reconstruction would thus run that there was a social change marked by the emergence of a concern for the individual, or rather a certain group of important individuals. The fact that there are female as well as male burials of the new type indicates that the individuals are a class, and not, for example, individuals singled out because of their particular attributes or achievements. The males of the class are distinguished in death by their possession of weapons, presumably indicating a continuation of an important aspect of their role in the life of the society.

An aspect of the ritualisation of warfare which can be observed in the weaponry is the choice of weapon types. In the earlier periods we find battle-axes and spears; later, spears become much less common and daggers and short swords are emphasised. We know that archery was well-known in the third and second millennia, but we almost never find metal arrowheads, which would be our archaeological indicator of the use of the bow, until the latter part of the second millennium. The change in the status of archery may be linked to the arrival of the horse-drawn chariot at about 1600 B.C. Up to that time archery was a rather low-status skill. The advent of the chariot introduced a new, very high-status and extremely expensive weapon of war, one sought by every ruler of the age. The chariot provided a mobile fighting-platform, and suddenly archery becomes prized because arrows were the ideal form of chariot-to-ground missile.

It is also interesting to use the details of weapon design as a cultural indicator. While there are various functional characteristics which can be identified as making up a 'good' battle-axe or an efficient spearhead, there is plenty of room for the exercise of cultural choice as to the weight, or the balance, or the applied ornament on a weapon, the details which no doubt made it 'right'. As well as being able to watch how fashions changed through time, it is also possible to map the distribution of particular weapon designs and see how they coincide with other cultural patterns. In the last centuries of the third millennium B.C. in the south of the Levant, for example, it appears that, within a general cultural homogeneity over the whole area, there were highly detailed local differences in the style of the main weapon, the dagger. Perhaps one could recognise important matters such as the affiliation or local origin of a man at that time by the dagger he wore.

Further weight is added to the idea that at certain periods appearance counted in these matters by the observation that a number of the weapons which are found in graves seem to be designed to look expensive and impressive. When we find them after several thousand years in the tomb, their organic parts, that is their hilts, have decayed. We can see that the attachment of the hilt to the blade was in some cases a good deal less strong than one would have wished if one's life depended on the dagger's effectiveness.

The discovery of glass

Glass is one of man's first fully synthetic products. Early man had worked flint, carved bone, woven baskets for thousands upon thousands of years, but none of these materials was synthesised. When mud was sun-baked into brick or clay was fired into pottery, the material was altered; but in the case of glass, sand and ash, and perhaps a metallic oxide as a colourant, are mixed and worked in the hot environment of a kiln to produce a new and quite different material. The processes involved in glass manufacture also require predictive and manipulative skills. Because of its physical structure glass is capable of seemingly endless variation and this is increasingly seen in its use today at home, in industry and even in space.

The invention of glass is usually placed in Egypt around 1500 B.C. and explained as the result of advances made by faience-workers. Faience comprised a silica body and a thin, glassy surface. The startling results of recent studies suggest that this standard explanation is in need of reappraisal.

Ethnographic observations and replication studies in the laboratory demonstrate that faience was worked in a cold state. Like pottery, the finishing process for faience is to bake it in a kiln. Glass, however, is worked in the hot state. The first stage in the history of glass is marked by occasional accidents in the formation of glazes, which can be traced back to about 3000 B.C. In the next stage, which begins about 1600 B.C., we see the first deliberate and consistent examples of true glass manufacture. The products of this stage are mould-made figurines, beads and core-formed vessels. The vessels are vividly coloured by the use of metal oxides. These elements – the use of moulds, the working of glass in a hot, viscous state, the use of metals for colourants – are all features of the established metal-working traditions. It now begins to seem that metal-workers were closely involved in the discovery of glass (just as it was blacksmiths in 1884 who invented rolled plate glass).

Thus it appears that, although some knowledge of glass existed from about 3000 B.C., the processes were first understood and controlled only some 1500 years later. The historical context of this technical breakthrough probably lies in N. Mesopotamia, what is now N. Syria. It occurred at exactly the time when a radically new aristocracy, named in the texts of the periods the Mitanni, appeared in that area. The conjunction was not fortuitous, it seems. The Mitanni re-structured native political and social traditions, and generated other technological innovations as well as glass with their demand for colourful new products of novel design for the purposes of conspicuous display.

The recurrence of such precious objects of novel technology in temples as well as in palaces suggests that the pyrotechnical innovations took place in the workshops attached to both these types of great institutions. In the international and cosmopolitan world of the Near East and the East Mediterranean of those times the knowledge of glass making quickly spread to Egypt and Mycenaean Greece.

Finger-printing clays to map the potters' markets.

Pottery has been much used by archaeologists for over a century, and it must puzzle many people why archaeologists continue to devote so much attention to so commonplace a material. The greatest part of the answer is that pottery was such a commonplace in people's lives in the past, and that its high survival value means that it is a valuable source of data to the archaeologist. There are many traditional ways in which pottery can be indicative for the archaeological enquirer, but in recent years two methods of analysis of the fabric of pottery have begun to yield important new kinds of information.

One of the approaches starts from the techniques of petrology within the field of geology. By slicing a thin section out of a piece of pottery, grinding it to such a thin-ness that it becomes translucent, and examining its structure under the microscope, it is possible for the petrologist, the specialist who can identify rocks from their individual crystals, to recognise the fine grit which the potter added to the clay to temper it. When we are lucky the grit can be related to a particular rock outcrop, and the approximate area of production of that pottery can be located on the map. (An example of this application lies behind the identification of Cornwall as the origin of some of the pottery found at neolithic Hambledon Hill in Dorset – see the piece on the Hambledon rituals of the dead in the following section.)

The other method of analysis involves nuclear physics, and requires access to the nuclear reactor. Neutron activation analysis (NAA) is a technique which measures the physical make-up of the clay which a potter has used. Minute samples drilled from potsherds are irradiated for a short time in a nuclear reactor, and are then placed in a counter. The radiation given off by the irradiated samples is counted and sorted by complex instruments. Each element present in the sample gives off a characteristic radioactive signal, and the tiny amounts of very · rare elements (measured in parts per million) are often the key variables between one clay source and another. The results of the physical analyses are then analysed statistically by computer to find groupings within the data. The statistical groups are pots made from the same clay and represent a particular potter or group of potters using a particular clay source. Sometimes it is even possible to go one step further and identify the locality of the clay source and thus of the potters who used it.

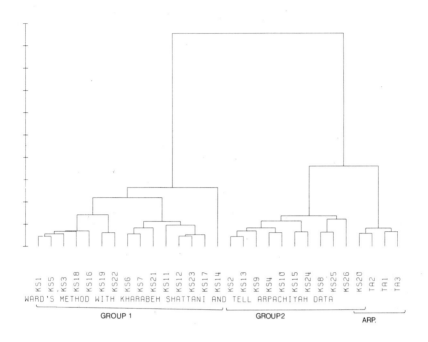

WARD'S METHOD WITH KHARABEH SHATTANI AND TELL ARPACHIYAH DATA

GROUP 1   GROUP2   ARP.

Fig 16. The computer illustrates by means of a dendrogram the groups of samples of related clays. The small groups at the right of the diagram consists of one sherd from the same site as all the other pottery and three sherds from another site (Arpachiya).

One area where the NAA technique has been applied is in the study of the economic infrastructure of a prehistoric people who lived in N. Mesopotamia six thousand and more years ago. It had been thought that industrialised production of goods and widespread trading in goods and raw materials began only with the arrival of urban civilizations such as that of southern Mesopotamia. But the so-called Halaf pottery of N. Mesopotamia would seem technically and artistically to imply the existence of · highly skilled groups of professional potters at a much earlier date. Halaf pottery has been recognised from sites as far apart as N. W. Iran and central Turkey, and for many years archaeologists have suspected that ·it was exported well beyond the extensive area of N. Iraq, N. Syria and S. E. Turkey where it was manufactured.

Now NAA has enabled archaeologists to identify with a very high statistical probability that sherds of Halaf pottery found outside its own cultural area were indeed exported. In some cases it has even been possible to identify the site where the exported pot was produced. The study of Halaf ceramics has also been concerned with the internal distribution or market in pottery within the Halaf culture area. Stylistically it has been easy to recognise that some Halaf pottery, a small minority, is of exceptionally high quality. Analysis of samples of pottery from two excavations at ordinary village sites in N. Mesopotamia, from surface-collected pottery from other sites, and from museum collections of material from old excavations has shown that the Halaf pottery industry and market was highly organised. At an Halaf culture site recently excavated as part of the archaeological salvage programme behind a dam on the Tigris in N. Iraq, the majority of the pottery was locally made. A minority of pottery, indistinguishable to the archaeologist's eye, was made of a rather different clay, and was probably supplied to the village from elsewhere. One single sherd in the sample analysed, a high quality piece, proved to be of the same clay as a known high-quality workshop.

The same kind of tiered structure was found at another village site excavated in N. Syria: the bulk of the material was locally manufactured in the village; some better quality pottery was supplied from a local centre; and a very small minority of high-quality pottery was made at specialist centres and very widely distributed across and beyond the whole cultural area. In the quest to understand something of the complex economic processes which later led to the emergence of literate, urban civilization in the Near East, a new way of looking at little sherds of pottery is enabling the humble potsherd to continue to play its important role in archaeology.

Experiments in bead-making

Beads are so commonplace and have been in use over so many thousands of years that we probably never stop to think how to drill the narrow hole through a stone bead, especially without the use of a metal drill bit. Combining evidence from contemporary ethnography, ancient illustrations and archaeological remains, it is possible to reconstruct the industry and replicate it.

At Jawa, a walled town in eastern Jordan dating to the late 4th millennium B.C., were found a great many flint drill bits made from roughly chipped water-rolled pebbles. Together with these was found a dense scatter of chipped carnelian, a lovely, translucent, orange-red semi-precious stone. There were also some partly drilled carnelian blanks, which showed that the finds represented the remains of bead factory. It is possible that similar techniques were in use at ancient Jawa. The drill bits from Jawa are very worn and smoothed at the tip. Carnelian is a very hard stone, and it is probable that an abrasive such as sand was used to improve the efficiency of the drill.

Other bead-making workshops have been discovered at nomadic encampment sites in the Jordan's Black Desert. The campsites belonged to hunters and herders who lived in the area about 8000 years ago. Unlike the Jawa bead-makers, they used thin slivers of flint as drill bits, and they collected soft pink and green stones to make into beads. Both types of stone were first worked into workable flakes. Once a flake had been perforated it was then reduced to a small disc-shaped, or a larger oval, bead.

There are two early types of drill, both still in use in some parts of the world. With the bow drill a strip of cord or leather is wound around the shaft which holds the drill bit, each end of the cord being attached to a curved stick or bow. As the bow is worked backwards and forwards the shaft is rotated by the cord. The torsion drill is more sophisticated. A flywheel is attached to the lower part of the shaft which holds the drill bit. The upper part of the shaft is inserted through a pierced bar which is suspended at either end by a cord. First the bar is spun so that the cords twist themselves around the shaft of the drill. When downward pressure is applied to the bar, the shaft of the drill rotates, and the flywheel causes the shaft to continue spinning until the cord is rewound. Another downward push spins the drill again and continues the process of unwinding and rewinding the cord.

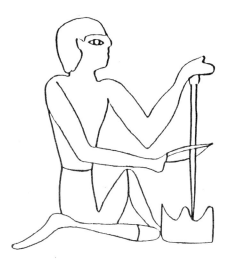

Fig 17. An ancient Egyptian representation of a man using a bow-
         drill.

Where it is possible, it is useful to test that one's analysis of the
remains of the past is plausible, and in this case careful copies of
beads which had been found on Early Bronze Age sites in Jordan
were manufactured using a bow drill with a flint bit. Beads from these
third millennium B.C. sites were made from white limestone and a
greenish blue steatite, and also shell and birds' leg bones. Chicken
bones were used in the modern replication experiment to make the
long spiral beads. The leg bones were cut into sections and then
incised using a flint chip. The edges of the ring beads were shaped
and finished by rubbing in fine sand.

Callanish Archaeological Research Centre, Lewis, Outer Hebrides

Immediately adjacent to the famous Callanish standing stones the former Callanish farm is now an archaeological research centre. The centre is still rather new, but its ambitious programme of work is gathering momentum. The research programme is designed to have three complementary and interlocking aspects, archaeological fieldwork (some of the excavations which form part of this aspect of the research are described in the earlier section on settlement), environmental studies and experimental work on agricultural economy and building technology. As the field centre programme unfolds, it is also planned to include an open air exhibition area and visitor facilities which will be developed in collaboration with local agencies as an educational and tourist investment in the region. In this section, however, we are concerned with the experimental work on agriculture using some of the 200 acres of land which form Callanish Farm.

Atlantic Scotland is exceptionally rich in field monuments of the prehistoric and early historic periods. The density, variety and stability of early settlement in the Outer Hebrides argues for a dependence upon a soundly based agricultural economy. The Callanish-based research is predominantly concerned with the Iron Age and early medieval period, roughly from the 7th century B.C. In order to understand the settlement history of this period, especially within the quite severe constraints imposed by the Hebridean climate and environment, we need to know a great deal more about the agricultural base.

The purpose of the agricultural experimentation is not to attempt to produce a version of the agricultural technology of a particular period and then watch it in action to see how it performs. We do not know enough about the farming practice of any particular period in the Outer Hebrides to begin to replicate it. Further, the present soils are certainly not the same as those of ancient times, so that simple replication would be impossible. And, within the long span of the island's prehistory and early history, it is very probable that environmental conditions as well as farming technology changed; to select one particular set of conditions and one form of farming practice for experimentation, even if that were possible, would eliminate the possibility of using the results in the interpretation of other periods.

The Callanish experimental agriculture starts from another direction. Most of the fields on the farm have never been used with modern herbicides, insecticides, or chemical fertilizers, so the soil conditions can be taken to be 'natural' for the present time. The first stage of experimentation involves growing traditional varieties of barley and oats under carefully monitored conditions. Having established the parameters of 'the normal' against such variations as rainfall and weather conditions from year to year, and soil drainage conditions in different parts of the fields, the experiment can move on to introduce variations on the normal in order to measure what effect they may have. The sort of variations which are to be introduced are such practices as weeding and manuring with seaweed..

In order to monitor the weather an automatic weather station has been installed in the fields. At predetermined intervals throughout each day the weather station's sensors' readings of air temperature, soil temperature, wind speed and direction, rainfall, relative humidity, solar radiation, and surface wetness are recorded. From time to time the recorded readings are downloaded to the centre's micro-computer; and from Callanish the archive of data is periodically transferred to the Edinburgh University's mainframe computers for compilation into the database and subsequent statistical analysis and plotting.

The cereal growing experiment is conducted to experimental guidelines laid down by the Scottish Schools of Agriculture. There are 12 experimental plots, each 7 metres square. Within each plot the one metre margin is excluded from the experiment in case of contamination from the surrounding area. This leaves a 5 metre square in each plot, from which random one metre squares can be chosen using a random number generation program on the Centre's micro-computer. The grain is sown at a uniform rate in drills to eliminate the possibility of birds taking seed sown on the surface. In the early stages of the experiment no attempts were made to interfere with natural weed growth; hand weeding will be another of the variations to be monitored carefully at a later stage. The crop is harvested by hand in September, five 1 metre squares being selected at random from each of the 12 plots. Even before the yields for each plot are measured it is clear that there are substantial variations in the quantities produced. It is also necessary to identify and count the weeds in each sample square in each plot.

Another planned experiment is concerned with pollen analysis. At present pollen analysts interpret their pollen counts according to a set of theoretical parameters; it is known, for example, that different species produce different quantities of pollen, and that pollens of different species vary in size and weight and are therefore airborne to different extents. The closely monitored experimental plots and weather conditions at Callanish provide a controlled background of pollen production and dispersion. By placing a series of collecting slides around the margins of the fields and comparing the various slides each season it will be possible to assess the relationship between what the pollen analyst sees on the slides and what was actually growing in the field.

The experimental agriculture programme will take many years to accomplish its objectives. There will be trials made of the use of different methods of cultivating the fields. There are different varieties of the basic crops of barley and oats to be tested, not to mention the extension of the programme to oth er species. At some stage animal husbandry will also be introduced to the pattern.

Reconstructing the Balbridie building, Deeside, Scotland

When the cropmark on Balbridie farm was discovered in the late 1970's it was at first thought to represent the foundations of a large, rectangular timber hall of the early historic period. Such timber halls had been found and excavated in England, particularly in the territory of the Anglian kingdom of Northumbria, and were reconstructed, partly on the basis of historical records, as the royal feasting halls of kings. When the Balbridie building was excavated it proved indeed to be the negative remains of a huge timber building, but the clear dating evidence was that it belonged more than 3000 years earlier than expected.

The uniqueness of the building posed special problems of interpretation of the excavated holes in the ground. The archaeologists could no longer appeal to the early medieval royal timber halls. Was the construction a roofed house at all? Elsewhere in Scotland there were instances of contemporary timber-built unroofed enclosures, including one with a double row of internal posts, intended for the ceremonial exposure of the dead.

The archaeologists had to try to analyse their excavation data in order to see if there were any clues to the nature and function of the construction. They started at a double disadvantage. In the first place all the structural timbers had completely decayed, and only the negative impressions of their bases were recovered, where they had been buried in the great post-pits and foundation trenches. In the second place the age- old cultivation of the field in which the site had once stood had ploughed away all trace of the floor level and anything which had once been on it. All that survived of what had been on the ground at the time that the structure stood was the carbonised grain and fragments of pottery which had trickled into the cavities left when the final fire had burned the timber posts and left the underground stumps to rot.

One clue that the timbers had been part of a single, load-bearing structure was observed in the way in which the posts had been very deeply bedded into the ground. The posts along the long sides had been buried to a depth of about one metre, and the two inner rows of posts were even more firmly set. It was also thought significant that there was a correspondence between the positions of posts set against the inner margins of the two long-side foundation trenches

Fig 18. The great timber building at Balbridie on Deeside under excavation.

and the two rows of great aisle-posts; this correspondence would indicate that the aisle-posts and the posts in the outer foundation trenches were elements in a unitary structure. And the greater depth of the settings of the major aisle-posts would also accord with their greater role as load-bearing elements.

A second clue was in the fairly well-preserved state of the pottery which was found in the post-pipes. Neolithic pottery was fired at relatively low temperatures and does not stand up well to long exposure to the elements. The sharp, unabraded edges of the pottery found at Balbridie suggested that it had been lying in a protected environment.

There are long, timber-built houses of a similar date known in wide areas of Europe, but the Balbridie house, if it were roofed, was about twice the width of the European examples. Seen as a unitary structure it supposes a very assured and considerable structural achievement for people using only stone tools. For example, the design rested the main weight of the roof on the two, widely-spaced rows of aisle-posts, leaving the centre of the floor entirely open, but also leaving the roof and its massive ridge-pole unsupported by a line of axial support posts.

Recalling that the angle of pitch of a thatched roof, whatever the material used, must be about 45 degrees, it is possible to use simple geometry to reconstruct the height of the peak of the roof above the ground. The first stage is to estimate the height of the side walls. These were framed on posts which were set one metre deep in the ground, and as a simple rule of thumb it is said that up to one third of a structural post will be earth-fast; thus the side walls can be reconstructed as having been two metres high, and the ridge-pole of the roof would then have been a full eight metres above the ground.

The investments of labour and skill put into the building are typified by the observations that a number of the massive, tree-trunk posts were shown to have been squared, and that the final, massive construction needed no external buttresses to relieve the thrust of the roof. The reconstruction of the Balbridie house indicates for the first time something of the level of wooden architecture attained by the cousins of the communities who built the better-known, stone-built, great ch ambered cairns.

Reconstructing a cist-grave, Dalgety, Fife.

In a later section the Early Bronze Age cemetery at Barns Farm, Dalgety, in Fife, is described as an example of how difficult it is to pin down the burial customs of a prehistoric society. One of the concerns of the investigating team was to learn something about the community which the cemetery represented.

Some of the burials were placed in carefully prepared, stone-built cists, which were closed with a massive stone lid. Each cist was set in a pit and was formed like a stone box made from slabs of stone. The normal cist was large enough to accommodate a tightly folded body lying on its side. It occurred to the excavators who had such close contact with the six cists excavated that even such apparently simple constructions must have involved some considerable input of community effort in their preparation and construction.

With the ready agreement of the headmaster of the local primary school, an experiment was set up one weekend in the grounds of his school. The stones of one of the cists were taken from the site to the school grounds, where a group of students and staff set to work on a carefully planned set of trials. The objective of the experiment was to estimate the minimum number of people who would have been needed to gather the stones and build the cist and the minimum time which the task would have required. The construction of the cist was broken down into a series of tasks. One task was to try ways of digging the pit for the construction of a cist, using technology appropriate to the period (approximately 4000 years ago, before metal became used for common tools). The big slabs of stone used in the construction of the cists had been brought to the cemetery from exposures some hundreds of metres away by the sea-shore. The two larger side-slabs weighed about 0.75 ton, and the capstone (which was not used in the experiment) was estimated to be 1.5 tons. Thus another task was to try ways of moving such stones in order to discover the best combination of man-power versus time. A further task was to assemble the slabs in the pit, again using only such tools and materials as would have been available at the period.

For the purpose of the experiment the group had assembled such equipment as wooden rollers, levers, antler picks, a shovel in the form of an ox scapula, baskets and rope. The most difficult aspect of the experiment was not in moving the big side-slabs, but in working out what was the most efficient (least number of people versus shortest time taken) solution. The massive–looking slabs in fact slid easily across the wooden rollers. The critical factor in this part of the test appeared to be the number of people available to manage the transfer of rollers from behind the stone to the front of the stone as it moved steadily forward. The team concluded, after many timed 'runs' with their stones under all sorts of combinations of people pulling and people managing the rollers, that four people could manage such a stone. However, in view of the much greater weight of the capstone, and bearing in mind the need to think of efficiency of time, they concluded that a team of eight would have been needed, at least for parts of the task.

Taking a team of eight as being effectively required for part of the job, it was possible to make minimum estimates of the total length of time the whole construction task would have taken. The answer came out as a rather surprisingly long period of more than three 10-hour working days. The experiment was useful in showing that even such a commonly found (in the North of Britain) type of single burial must represent the input of several days of hard physical work, and that an extensive group of people, wider than the immediate family, would have needed to cooperate in the common task of burial.

There was another consequence of the experiment. A school in Fife has the unique distinction of being able to list amongst its physical teaching resources an original, Early Bronze Age cist.

Vitrified ramparts, the burning question

Experiment with archaeologically known buildings is focussed mainly on problems of construction, for which, especially in the case of ancient timber buildings, much of the problem is occasioned by the paucity of the surviving evidence. In the case of vitrified ramparts there has always been plenty of good, solid evidence, and the problem has been one of ambiguity over the interpretation.

Vitrified forts, though they represent only a small minority of the total of known hill-forts, have been clearly recognised since the 18th century. The stone of which the rampart was mainly formed had obviously been subjected to intense heat to the extent that it had begun to liquify and resolidify in a somewhat glassy form. In some forts the vitrified portions of the rampart were confined to only a part of the wall's circuit, while in others practically the whole extent was vitrified.

Archaeological opinion remains divided on one central issue: this may be called the 'construction versus destruction argument'. Were these vitrified walls, typified by solid masses of fused stonework, designed to be so? In other words, was the timber framework intended simply to provide the combustion which would solidify the newly built rampart? If so, was it necessary to add an extra ingredient to act as a fluxing agent to raise the very high temperatures necessary to melt the rocks? Or, on the other hand, are the vitrified ramparts we see the remains of destruction, whether deliberate or accidental?

Geological knowledge and laboratory experiments have shown that the necessary temperatures were of the order of 1000 degrees Celsius, and scientists have been sceptical that such temperatures would have been induced simply by setting fire to such fortifications as the archaeologists reconstruct on paper from their excavation experience. The use of some extra ingredient which might have improved the combustibility of the rampart would have supported the view that vitrification was conceived as a sophistication of construction. But no-one has ever been able to identify beyond reasonable doubt any additional materials other than stone and timber.

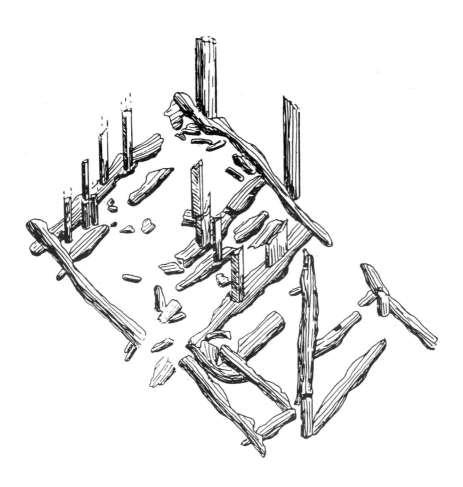

Fig 19. *The recovered timbers of the framework of the vitrified rampart of Green Castle, Portknockie.*

Half a century ago Professor Gordon Childe had considered the practicalities of vitrification in the light of the burning of a scale model of such a wall in the grounds of Plean Colliery, Stirlingshire. The opportunity to construct a stretch of full scale timber-laced rampart with a view to igniting it as a controlled experiment in vitrification was recently provided by Yorkshire Television, who offered to fund and film the experiment.

94

The burning of the Yorkshire Television wall produced small quantities of altered stonework, which subsequent geological examination indicated must have reached approximately 950 degrees, very close to the predicted temperature of 1000 degrees. The television experiment had to be brought to a close after 30 hours of burning. At that time it was found that there were quantities of the pine timber lacing incompletely consumed and still burning. Taken with the archaeological observation that in most cases the evidence for burning is found round only a part of a fort's circuit, the results of the experiment support the destruction model rather than the construction hypothesis.

Situated in some cases on conspicuous hill-tops, the burning of the timber-laced ramparts of such forts must have proffered a spectacular intimation of the victor's destructive power. Burning for several days on end, glowing orange and red against the night sky, with the stonework cracking under the intense heat, such walls would have impressed a never to be forgotten image of defeat in the memory of the vanquished, an impression which could only have been reinforced by the sight of the blackened and vitrified results in the cold light of later days.

Section 4: The archaeology of society and belief

Much of the time when archaeologists are dealing with the sites of former settlements, or the fragmentary remains of what was used in everyday life, the people who lived on the site and made and used the objects we find are absent. When archaeologists can excavate a cemetery they are closer to the people in a literal sense.

The physical remains of the dead can give a surprising amount of information about their former lives. The expert can determine the sex and physical size of the person and their approximate age at death. Some accidents and diseases leave clear traces on the bones, and sometimes even hints as to the diet and level of nutrition can be learned. Taken together as statistics, the bodies from a cemetery can give an idea of the population structure and life expectancy of a community.

The way the dead are buried can also tell us a good deal about the society in which they lived and its beliefs, especially as many ancient societies buried their dead with more ceremony than is customary in our own times. In particular the objects which commonly accompany the burial may indicate something of the status or rank of the person, or the wealth and power of the family group who buried their dead relative. A hierarchically organised society may mirror its pyramidal structure in the differentiation of the provision for its dead. An ethnically heterogeneous society may reveal itself in the variety of burial rites or the variety of provision of grave-goods.

Archaeology is poor in its ability to deal with the unique or the personal: archaeological data derives from the commonplace and people as groups rather than as individuals. Archaeology is better at the resolution of the macro-level rather than the micro-level. Thus it is very difficult to deal with the social position of the individual through archaeological means, even though we may have the very physical remains of an individual in a particular grave. It is easier to look at the whole cemetery, to look for patterns and analyse its structure through statistics, in the search for the broad warp and weft of large-scale social organisation. We may have in an excavation the house in which a particular family or household lived over a period of generations, and we may be able to determine the different functions of the various rooms and courtyards: but we shall find it practically impossible to discern the form of kinship or other inter-personal relations which bound that household into an organic body. We should do better to look at the broader canvas of the patterning of houses, streets, storage facilities, industrial areas, central public buildings and religious monuments, in short the settlement archaeology, if we wish to learn something of the social conditions of life in an extinct community.

At many times and in many parts of the world societies have raised monuments as indications of their deeply held common beliefs or tokens of their common aspirations. We see something of this common cultural phenomenon in our own society, where, we are told, the creation of a new museum or art gallery has become a major concern of any city aspiring to a central place in the cultural world. Others might point to the competition between commercial institutions and cities with a concern for their image as important centres for trade and commerce to build taller, more flamboyant and more assertively opulent company headquarters in city centres. A similar kind of civic pride can be seen at a slightly earlier stage in the deliberately monumental and public architecture of schools; and once universities, before they fell from grace, were sometimes termed 'temples of learning'. Just as alien archaeologists would find our medieval cathedrals difficult to interpret in terms of the Christian liturgy for which they were the arena, so we find the system of beliefs which a henge or a stone circle housed and symbolised may remain beyond our ability to recapture. Nevertheless we can at least measure something of that society's ability to mobilise its resources of wealth and manpower in such massive constructions, and we may also see something of their enduring importance in the way that these monuments were maintained and reshaped often over many centuries.

The archaeology of society and the archaeology of social systems of belief and ideology, it has to be remembered, are relatively new fields, into which archaeologists have only recently begun to venture with any sense of deliberate exploration. Systematic archaeology as a means of exploring the past is arguably only about a century old, three or four generations of scholarship. The notion of human culture itself, and the relationship between the things we make and use as 'material culture' and the quite abstract concept of culture in general began to be explored only in the second quarter of this century. At the mid-point of the century many prehistoric archaeologists were convinced that, although social, political and ideological aspects were necessarily involved even in humble material culture, it was beyond the ability of archaeology to disentangle such complex and abstract threads from a starting point in pottery, architecture or other common artefacts. Only in the the decades since the mid- to late 1960's have archaeologists, at first a minority, begun to take a more optimistic and holistic view. Even so,

Fig 20. A modern addition to the repertoire of motifs carved on the black rocks of the Jordanian desert – but what does it mean?

the task of disentangling the complex threads of intention, function, technology and meaning around common artefacts requires a level of theoretical or general understanding of how human culture and society operates which still eludes us. Much current theoretical research and discussion revolves around the difficult problems of the higher levels of interpretation of common artefacts. As yet the achievements may be few and rather puny, but these are early days and the mills of scholarship grind with a less-than-divine slowness.

Culture, history and the processes of change

Is there more to archaeology than the excitement of discovery, the curiosity of the antique? The archaeologist would say yes: because of the way in which archaeology explores the relationship between things and our cultural lives, it is showing that there is a language in artefacts just as there is a language of literature, or music, a 'text' to be discerned in a film, or a body language. The exploration of the past throws light on the present in a way quite different from that of the historian. Archaeologists are in one sense concerned with the past in the way that historians are: the archaeologist may be able to throw light on the history of metallurgy, or the evolution of architectural style, or the pattern of everyday life in Viking York in ways which every historian would recognise.

The archaeologist has access to all sorts of information which was never recorded in the documents studied by the historian; in historical periods the work of the archaeologist is complementary to that of the historian. We know, for example, from the surviving works of Latin historians when the Roman legions were despatched to conquer Britain, which legions they were and who led them. The Latin sources, however, are very imprecise as to how the campaigns were carried out, how the frontier zone was managed, or how the process of conversion to a civil province of the Roman Empire came about: information about such matters must be sought in the field, in the network of Roman military roads supporting the forts, in the physical evidence of the disposition of forces on the linear frontier of Hadrian's Wall or the Antonine Wall. The historian cannot reach back in time beyond the earliest literate societies except in terms of the physical record. In Britain there is no written record earlier than the first coming of the Romans; and nowhere in the world is there documentary data for the historian to study earlier than about 3000 BC. Human prehistory, however, is immensely longer than that (several hundred times longer than the maximum historical period, in fact), and the archaeologist alone can penetrate these remote periods, to chart the thousands and tens of thousands of years of early human cultural and social development.

For the vast expanse of human prehistory archaeology is our only source of information, and the huge time-scale offers archaeology the opportunity to explore the processes of cultural evolution and economic and social development which seem to us to be fundamental to our present way of life. The penalty of archaeological data is that it leaves the people of prehistory impersonal and anonymous: the advantage of prehistoric archaeology is in the great time-scale within which we can study the slow but vital processes which have culminated in the major transformations of human society.

Questions of how processes have unfolded which are currently attracting much attention among archaeologists are such questions as how people first evolved the way of life which we consider to be basic to our own life-style, life in permanent settlements based on the production of food by farming (as opposed to the more fluid social relations and temporary encampments of the classic hunter-gatherers); how social and economic inequalities became institutionalised in human society, leading to hierarchically organised, economically complex societies; how technical advances such as the knowledge of metals and the mastery of alloying were discovered, disseminated and used in non-utilitarian ways by various societies; how urbanism first arose; how the earliest political states emerged. In all of these subjects the unexpected results of research into cultural and historical contexts which are completely alien to our own experience stimulate fresh responses to aspects of our human condition; in turn that leads to a deeper understanding of the nature of human society and a keener appreciation of our context within the scale of human history.

The anonymity of prehistory has required archaeologists to contemplate the communities they study not in terms of their language and literature, their names and their individual deeds, but in terms of their buildings, their graves, their pots, their ornaments, weapons, food debris and tools. Slowly archaeologists have constructed their own version of the concept of human culture, the shared codes of belief and practice which enable to live our sociable lives. Archaeologists have access to these shared ideas, beliefs and practices only through the medium of the the artefacts which are their material product. At first archaeologists saw artefacts as indicators of time; later they began to recognise that a certain artefact might seem to characterise or typify the people who lived at a certain time in a particular area. In the second quarter of the 20th century Gordon Childe developed this idea of a typical artefact as a label for a particular group of people into a typical set of artefacts, the concrete or material culture aspect of people who share abstract cultural patterns of belief and common practices.

The 'new archaeology' movement of the 1960's and 1970's concentrated on the theory of culture and affirmed the systematic relationship between all aspects of cultural life and all the artefacts which people make. Optimistic young archaeologists insisted that the cautious empiricism of earlier archaeologists was unnecessarily utilitarian and narrowly functionalist; it was axiomatic in their view that all aspects of human culture found expression in action and in artefacts, including such abstract aspects as how we see our society as being ordered, how we see our political and social relations within our community or between peoples, and how we see our human world as related to the wider natural world and the cosmos in general. The problem for the archaeologist became one of not being at all sure what was the grammar of the cultural language of artefacts. For ourselves, viewing our own cultural context, we might can accept that our world is full of artefacts which abound in messages; for the most part we 'read' these messages without thinking about them as we go about our daily lives, but we only need to take conscious note and a walk down the street can become an exercise in the analysis of artefacts, static and portable, and their non-verbal cultural language. But intuitively we can also recognise that the cultural language of our experience need not be a universal language.

In recent years one important area of archaeological research has been in the theoretical exploration of the material 'language' of culture. Researchers have taken to the field to study how contemporary societies articulate cultural ideas through the medium of their artefacts. The longterm goal of these 'ethno-archaeologists' is to elucidate the general rules which govern the relationships between the material and the non-materials of culture. Another aspect of this move to study the relationship between the common ideas, concepts, beliefs and customs and things is the delving into dustbins, the analysis of the trashcans, whereby a major research project at the University of Arizona is engaged in monitoring how the local citizens deal with their waste. As archaeologists have become more and more aware of the complexity of human cultural attitudes to material things, they have also recognised more clearly that what the archaeologist is looking at is not, as it were, a photograph of life as it was, but a picture of life severely distorted by the way in which people in the past discarded, disposed of or abandoned the artefacts which we use to interpret their way of life. It is in fact very rare for the archaeologist to come across a picture of life as it was. The most famous example must be the Roman city of Pompeii, where life came to a sudden stop when the whole area was overwhelmed and completely buried by volcanic ash. There we find things where they were hastily abandoned as people fled. Usually the archaeologist is confronted with a very different picture in which we are vouchsafed only such broken and abandoned things as were discarded where we might find them; all sorts of other things were perhaps too important or precious to be simply thrown away, and yet other material may have been considered 'dirty' and have required to be disposed of in ways which remove it from our archaeological view.

Barns Farm, Dalgety.

The cemetery of graves which were found on Barns Farm, at Dalgety on the southern shore of Fife, constitute something of a cautionary tale. Since the time when Gordon Childe first formulated the theory of culture as the shared systems of belief and practice which bind us together, archaeologists have considered burial practice as another of the distinguishing cultural characteristics which we can use to label cultural groups. And burial practice, many have thought, should have a deeper cultural significance than, for example, the way we make knives and the shape of our drinking cups, since burial relates closely and directly to the belief systems of a people, what they believe about death and the hereafter, and how they regard the dead person.

Usually cistgraves are discovered singly, but sometimes, as at Dalgety, one cist leads to others. In fact at Dalgety there were six stone-built cists at various points on the close together on the top of a small and inconspicuous rounded hill. Four of the cists contained the expected single, inhumed skeleton, but one cist by contrast was much smaller than the others and was filled with cremated bone. Since all the cists had been sealed below a round burial mound they presumably belonged to one period and a single tradition.

The first cist provided an even more pointed combination. On its floor of selected and carefully laid white pebbles there lay the skeleton of a young man. In one corner of the cist there was also a pile of cremated remains, the fragmented and distorted bones of another individual. Such combinations of a cremation and an inhumation have been recorded before, but it had been generally believed that the cremation burial had been inserted into the cist at some secondary date. At Dalgety there was good reason to believe that the cist, made to accommodate a tightly contracted inhumation, had never been re-opened until the day a modern ploughshare pulled aside the cap-stone.

Cists were not the only form of burial at Dalgety. Three simple graves were also found. One of them had been badly damaged by ploughing and little can be said of it or its original contents. The other two were relatively long and narrow, quite different in proportions from the rather short cists. In all three graves the body had been laid at the bottom of the grave pit in a coffin made of some organic material which had decayed to such an extent that nothing was left beyond some stained soil. In the case of one of the coffins laboratory analyses and experiments suggested that the material was leather. The resemblance in shape of the coffin to a boat may thus be explained in terms of the coffin having once been a skin-clad boat of the coracle type.

Fig 21. The tightly folded body of a woman lies with her grave goods on the white pebble floor of a stone cist. At her knees is a broken pot, and below her chin are the tiny beads of jet necklace.

All three of the graves had also contained cremated remains as well as body lying on the floor of the coffin. The body in the coracle-coffin was accompanied by a sack of cremated remains by his feet; a second grave contained no less than three cremations besides the inhumed body. Whatever the details of the coffins and the graves which contained them, they introduce a further question: why were some people buried in a cist, while others were buried in a small boat re-used as a coffin and placed in a simple grave?

Archaeologists have also tended to think rather loosely about the purpose of artefacts found in graves with the remains of the dead, calling them by the general label 'grave goods'. Things placed with the dead may in different circumstances have quite different connotations. It may be necessary to provide the recently dead with some equipment for the after-life or the next world; or it may be the custom to place with the dead things which were precious or in some sense special to that person in life; or again it may be the custom for those attending the funeral to place with the dead tokens of their respectful presence and participation in the rites of death.

All three types of grave goods can be identified in different burials at Dalgety, showing that we should not assume that only one practice can be in use at one time. For example, one of the cists contained the remains of woman, who was buried wearing a necklace of jet beads, presumably some precious possession of her own. A pot of a type which is commonly thought to be a ritual form to be used in the life of the next world had been placed near her knees. Also in the cist were found two broken jet pendants. From their positions it was clear that the corpse had worn neither of them, and indeed it appears that they were thrown into the grave. Each had been deliberately snapped in two, and one half only of each was present in the grave, as if two mourners had broken pendants in order to keep one half and leave the other half with the dead.

The long burial mounds of North Europe

The megalithic tombs of Atlantic Europe became a very prominent focus of interest and research many years ago. The large mounds were prominent in the landscape, and the dark, narrow doorways to the silent burial chambers beneath the mound cried out for investigation. Less well known is a related series of long burial mounds, some in the east of Britain, and others widely spread over a huge area of northern Europe. These earthen mounds are externally blank, with no facades or doorways, and no internal chambers

Study of the European mainland series has been hampered by the lack of an overview, made very difficult because of their international distribution. Stretching east from the Netherlands and West Germany, the unchambered earthen mounds are also found in East Germany and Poland, and north into Denmark. From the excavations of these mounds which have been undertaken since the early 19th century the same sort of finds have always emerged, typified by a particular type of funnel- necked beaker. Besides the omnipresent pottery there were often some other, more interesting finds, such as polished stone battle-axes and maceheads, beads of shell, amber and copper. These were the burial mounds of small farming communities which inhabited this vast area from the late 4th millennium B.C. and through the 3rd millennium. Recently the accumulated information about these mounds was collected and studied by a research student, and the research was written up as a doctoral dissertation.

While these burial mounds have long exerted a fascination for local antiquarians and archaeologists, they have remained reluctant to yield their secrets. The smallest barrows may be 30 metres long, and the longest reach up to 170 metres. In plan they are rectangular, or more often trapezoidal or triangular. Their original height can be estimated to have been 2 or 3 metres. It is an irony that such conspicuous monuments, which were clearly meant to make an impressive statement in their landscapes, should be so difficult for us to understand.

In many cases the burial mounds are found to have been constructed on the site of a former settlement. Between the abandonment of the settlement and the building of the mound, however, there are two other stages of activity. Under the mound are found the burials, which, in contrast with the size of the mounds, are usually very few. With the burial there might be placed a few choice items from the list outlined above, evidence perhaps that those selected for this special treatment in death were of special status within their family or community. Around the mound there would be a stone kerb or traces of an enclosing fence of timber. These kerbs or fences should not be understood as retaining the mound, however, for there is evidence in a number of cases that the mound was a secondary construction which effectively buried an already existing enclosure.

It is frustrating that the archaeologists can outline in some detail the sequence of events, but there is almost no clue as to what the events meant to the people who built the enclosures in their abandoned settlements, buried their dead, and finally erected the huge earthen mounds.

One of the most recently and extensively excavated, and best-documented examples of the North European long barrow phenomenon is at Sarnowo in central Poland. Like many of the earthen mounds, the nine barrows at Sarnowo formed a clearly organised group. It is quite common to find barrows carefully arranged with their long sides parallel. The Sarnowo burial mounds were constructed not very long after the settlement was abandoned, for the remains of hearths and rubbish pits were still clear. Presumably the houses themselves were cleared out of the way to permit the change of use of the area to burials. First a stone-kerbed enclosure was built, and within each enclosure between one and five bodies was buried, the dead being placed in timber coffins which were then surrounded by piles of stones. Finally the earthen mound itself was constructed.

Perhaps it was the important members of a family or kinship group who were placed in these enclosures in a village of the dead. The final act of piety, possibly expressing the continuing social cohesion and solidarity of the group, was the erection of a massive monument over the ancestors.

Sarnowo poses one final enigma. There is no sign that these 'houses of the dead', if that is what they were, mirrored in form the houses which had formerly stood on that same site. Instead, and quite inexplicably, there is an obvious resemblance between earthen long barrow plans and the plans of houses of a contemporary nearby settlement of another cultural tradition.

Hambledon Hill: the mysteries of symbolic and ritual activity.

The large and complicated fortified settlement on Hambledon Hill has already been mentioned in the context of the vivid witness to very early warfare of its burned ramparts and slain defenders. Another aspect of the investigation concerns the plentiful evidence of (to our eyes) peculiar and apparently ceremonial activities of those who inhabited the enclosure around 2700 B.C. It has to be remembered that the interior of the enclosure had been terribly damaged both by natural erosion and by cultivation over more than four millennia. In consequence there were no surviving traces of structural remains, and whatever domestic refuse or industrial waste had once been lying on the surface was entirely gone.

In that portion of the interior which was excavated, however, there were the bottoms of more than 90 pits, many of which produced completely unexpected information which is very difficult to interpret. The cylindrical pits had been deliberately refilled, and in the soil were included certain categories of well-defined objects.

Red deer antlers, uncommon elsewhere on the site, occur in these pits in relatively large quantities, and are often at least partly scorched or burnt. Pots were also found in the fills of the pits, and, although they were recovered broken into many pieces, it is clear that they were often whole when they were deposited. Petrological analysis of the grits which were used to temper the clay of the pots shows that these pots were very special: they had originated on the Lizard peninsula at the extreme south-west of Cornwall. Yet other exotic objects were placed in pits, such as quern fragments which the geologist can show originated near Exeter, stone axes which came from quarries near St Ives in Cornwall, and even two axes, one of jadeite, the other of nephrite, which had been brought from Brittany.

The silted fill of the encircling ditches was a natural choice of deposit to dig, especially on an eroded and damaged site, but it soon became clear that the ditches concealed evidence of more strange activities relating in some way to the lives of the users of the enclosure. As the ditches began to silt up very special deposits began to be made. Human skulls, or parts thereof, had been placed irregularly all along the floor of the ditch. Since none of the 37 human crania that were recovered in the excavation of the ditch was found with any trace of the lower jaw, it would seem that the skulls were defleshed before deposition. There were other parts of human skeletons found in the ditch bottom among the skulls, but never enough to 'match' the occurrence of skulls. When further detail could be ascertained, it only serves to deepen the riddle. For example, in one particular instance analysis of the soil sediments inside one of the crania showed that the skull had been lifted after its original deposition and carefully replaced the other way up.

Alongside and around the cranial deposits there were further carefully placed heaps (probably originally the contents of sacks or bags all trace of which has decayed), which were all that remained of masses of organic material including more human bone, animal bone, pottery and flint-working debris. The animal bone is of particular interest because it comprises whole joints of prime meat, with the bones in complete articulation; the implication is that they had been deposited with meat and cartilage still intact on the bone. Such 'wastage' is very uncommon in contemporary subsistence farming societies: when it does occur it is often associated with 'feasting' or other events of conspicuous consumption when the very act of wastage is socially and economically significant.

At a later stage, when the ditch was rather more silted, the complete bodies of two young children were laid in the ditch and covered with cairns of flint. In the south-east sector of the enclosure another skeletal group of quite different significance was found. This comprised the lower trunk and thighs of an adolescent male, whose body had been gnawed by dogs or wolves. The gruesome reconstruction of events would be that the animals had dragged a decaying cadaver into the shelter of the ditch, losing the upper parts and the lower legs on the way. There is other evidence from other sites to show that excarnation, the exposure of the corpse to the elements (and worse) to hasten the removal of flesh from the skeleton, was part of the funerary practice in neolithic times in Britain.

It would seem that the interior of the enclosure at Hambledon Hill was set aside for the exposure and excarnation of human corpses. Six or seven hundred different bodies are represented among the fragmentary skeletal remains recovered from the partial excavations of the ditch; on that basis it is probable that thousands of bodies were laid out within the enclosure over the long period of its use. Another part of the practices that accompanied the funerary rituals was the digging of pits in which a significant and special set of artefacts was then buried. After excarnation some at least of the skeletal remains were placed in the ditch, and more again somehow found their way to the same place in bags of strangely assorted contents.

Having so many (partial) examples of the neolithic population of Hambledon, it is possible to learn something of their living conditions. There is an approximate balance between male and female skeletons in the sample, which encourages us to think that the sample may be fairly representative. About 60% of the bodies represent people who died as children or young adults, clear evidence of the much lower life expectations of the period. In the search for prevalent endemic diseases, we must bear in mind that only a few diseases will have left traces on the bones of the dead. Those who survived to reach adulthood were robustly built and of good stature, although they frequently exhibit traces of arthritis and related conditions, whose incidence was probably magnified by constant hard work and poor living conditions. The skulls of children in a number of instances show that they died of a terrible affliction in which the sutures of the skull knitted prematurely, thus inhibiting normal brain development. This is a condition related to rickets and is a product of dietary deficiency.

Most of the other information we have concerning the funerary practices of the neolithic period in Britain have come from the excavation of chambered tombs and unchambered long barrows; these monuments belong to the earlier part of the neolithic period. When the chambers or mortuary structures within these great burial mounds are excavated they are found to contain the remains of as many as 57 individuals. The skeletal material is frequently disarticulated, and often parts of skeletons are missing, suggesting that the bodies had already been exposed and excarnated, and that the bones were recollected in rather poor condition.

Within the long barrows, which belong in the earlier phase of the neolithic, there would appear to be a significant preference in favour of males and against females, while the remains of children are rather rarely encountered. This is a picture quite at variance with that portrayed at Hambledon. Putting the evidence of Hambledon and the long barrows together, perhaps we should conclude that after a period of excarnation in enclosures like Hambledon certain bodies were selected for burial within the great long burial mounds on the basis of achieved rather than inherited status, and according to a system which favoured males. Recent work on the long barrows of southern England indicates that the later tombs contain the remains of fewer and fewer individuals; the occupants become even more exclusively male, and they are often buried accompanied by prestigious objects indicative of their special status (a feature absent from the long barrows of the earlier neolithic).

The story of Hambledon Hill is long, complex and often obscure. In this account we see the interim statement of a study which is still in progress at the time of writing. From the evidence of Hambledon set against the information form the long barrows and their burials we can see that neolithic society already differentiated a minority as requiring additional and special treatment in death. Over the many centuries of the neolithic period we can begin to appreciate that, as its burial practices reflect, society was changing towards one in which a smaller and smaller segment of males were perceived as demanding greater and greater input of effort in the provision of monumental burial mounds. And the objects of special significance on account of their exotic origin or craftsmanship of rare quality, which were once buried in the communal excarnation enclosures such as Hambledon, are later found as the personal attributes of individuals, perhaps an emergent ruling group.

At present we still see very poorly into this distant and thoroughly unfamiliar society of neolithic times. All we can do is to formulate hypotheses which account for the facts as we see them at present, and confidently expect that new evidence from future excavation and study will require us to modify our ideas as well as refine them.

Pithekoussai, a Western Greek cemetery on Ischis, Italy

The first Greeks who ventured westwards at the end of the Dark Age were Euboeans. They were trading with the indigenous Iron Age peoples on the mainland of Tyrrhenian Italy by the first half of the eighth century B.C. It was not long before a permanent trading station (known in Greek as an emporion) was established on the island of Ischia at the northern end of the Bay of Naples. It is becoming increasingly clear that this hitherto little-known centre, which is rarely mentioned in the ancient written sources for Greek history, acted as a major clearing-house for the advanced technology and new ideas of all kinds brought to Italy from Greece. At the same time Greeks, among them the Euboeans, were themselves eagerly absorbing ideas and fashions from the Near East, where they were well represented in the multi-national emporion of Al Mina on the coast of Syria. Thus the 'Orientalizing' influences so keenly appreciated by the Greeks were transferred to the local cultures of Campania, Latium and Etruria through the Euboean centre of Pithekoussai on Ischia.

The large-scale transmission of culture and technology from the Aegean to the central Mediterranean was of incalculable and permanent significance for Western European civilization. And the investigation of Pithekoussai itself has been exceptionally prolific in historical, social and economic information. The excavation has been going on for 35 years; in the first volume of the publication of the excavations in the cemetery, which is currently in press, having taken almost 20 years in the preparation, are accounts of the first 723 graves. Of these almost 500 belong in the exciting formative period between about 750 and 700 B.C.

Since so little survives in the written record about this early Greek emporion, the archaeological record is of fundamental importance, and the graves of its early inhabitants constitute a priceless record of a remarkable episode. Clearly Pithekoussai acted as a magnet for entrepreneurs from many parts of the Greek world and also from other parts of the Mediterranean and the Levant.

After many years of excavation of the tombs in the cemetery and analysis of the gravegoods with which some of the burials were provided, it is possible to discern many aspects of structure within the cemetery which seem to reflect quite closely the structure of the society of Pithekoussai. For example, it is possible to discern the development of a family plot in the cemetery. Graves of one family cluster together. Because the stylistic development of the Greek pottery in use at Pithekoussai is so relatively well known, it is possible to apply a refined set of dates to graves containing pots and arrange graves in relative chronology. The precision of the dating of a set of pots may be as close as five to ten years.

The normal rite was cremation, and the cremated remains were then placed under a cairn, with or without grave-goods. As is quite common in cultures other than our own, babies and young children were treated differently from the adult dead. At Pithekoussai the young dead were not cremated, but were simply inhumed; nevertheless their status within the kinship group might still make the inclusion of grave-goods appropriate. A baby might be buried in an amphora. Some adults also failed to rate cremation and a cairn, and were buried without grave- goods.

Common among the grave-goods were small pots recognised as what were called by the Greeks aryballoi. These were the containers of sweet-smelling unguents used in preparing the corpse for the cremation ceremony, and they were then often buried with the cremated remains. All sorts of other pottery might be included among the grave-goods. While much of the pottery is recognisible as Euboean, the Pithekoussans also expressed their catholic tastes by importing pottery from other centres, notably Corinth and Rhodes.

The cemetery of Pithekoussai is also of very great interest because a very few of the objects found in graves were inscribed. In the Greek world at that period, close to the time of Homer, writing was only just beginning to be used again, after several centuries of illiteracy. One particularly interesting inscription, uncharacteristically long and literary, was incised on a drinking cup which had been made in Rhodes just before 720 B.C. The alphabet is typical of Chalcis in Euboea, and the latter two lines of the three line text are in perfect epic hexameters, exactly as the poetry of Homer. It is thus one of the oldest examples of Greek writing (leaving aside the Mycenaean Bronze Age Linear B script) that has survived anywhere; and it is nothing less than a piece of poetry of Homeric times, uniquely preserved in its contemporary script.

Most of the inscriptions are much more terse, however, but their interest for the composition of the population of Pithekoussai can nevertheless be considerable. One example is the inhumation of an infant buried in a coarse amphora which dates to about 740 B.C. On the amphora was scratched a four- letter word and a number, the oldest extant writing found to date on Italian soil. The script and the language of the inscription are Aramaic or Phoenician, both of which were in use in the Syrian and Lebanese coastlands with which Euboea was in touch. In such a personal matter as this inscription, surely, the indication is that the family of the dead baby were themselves Levantine.

Fig 22.   "Nestor had a most drinkworthy cup, but whoever drinks from this cup will soon be smitten with desire for fair-crowned Aphrodite."

The oldest post-Mycenaean Greek writing to survive is in Euboean script on a cup made in Rhodes found in a grave at Pithekoussai.

Rullion Green, Mid-Lothian, Scotland

The reason for investigating the long-known archaeological site at Rullion Green in the foothills of the Pentland Hills a few miles south of Edinburgh was that, despite being known for a couple centuries and in spite of being partly excavated some years ago, it was still a matter of debate as to whether the site was a very unusual kind of unenclosed settlement of small circular houses or a quite unique form of cemetery of circular burial monuments. About half of the site was dug between 1983 and 1985, and the first conclusion of the exercise was that the settlement idea had to be scrapped. There were no indications that the circular constructions were ever roofed, and they had no internal fittings or any domestic debris which could support their reconstruction as the remains of a group of houses.

There were clear signs that the site had been repeatedly used for highly elaborate rites connected with the disposal of human remains, and the difficulty of assigning a date to the site seems to have been resolved by a mid-first millennium B.C. radiocarbon date. But simply to call the site a cemetery overrates the role of the human remains and underplays the amount of ritually directed construction activity. In the end it appears that we do not have a word in English (or a concept in our cultural vocabulary) to convey the nexus of ideas and activities represented at prehistoric Rullion Green.

Each circular monument had at its centre a deposit of cremated human bone, but it was clear that the act of cremation had taken place elsewhere. What was found in each circle was some portion of the collected and carefully sorted residue from the cremation pyre. Different cremation deposits might be of quite variable quantities, and in quite different conditions; it is certain that most, if not all, of the cremation deposits are only token collections from the pyre, and that the collected bone was in some cases deliberately further reduced to very tiny, broken fragments.

A circle of ground about 6 metres in diameter was prepared to receive the token cremation deposit by being stripped of topsoil. A layer of clean subsoil was placed like a floor on the surface of the stripped disc of ground, and around the perimeter of the disc, perhaps to demarcate it, was dug a shallow ditch. The first of the peculiarities appears at this stage in the process, for the soil and subsoil which were dug out in the formation of the circular ditch are missing from the site. Every circle excavated proved to have a slightly different interpretation of the necessary activities and the sequence in which they should be conducted beyond these initial steps. One of the circles is described here to convey a general idea of the pattern of activities concentrated on the circular monuments, but no other circle is exactly like it in detail.

Around the inner edge of the ditch in (almost) every circle was found a small bank. In every case it can be shown that the ditch was not constructed from material dug from the ditch, as would have seemed the simplest way to form a bank and ditch. Indeed in the circle chosen for description here it can be shown that the ditch had been filled almost to the brim before the bank was built. Just as the soil and subsoil which had been removed to form the ditch was taken away from the site, so the sand and grit with which the ditch was refilled was brought from somewhere else for it is clearly different from the coarse gravel and cobbles of the local subsoil. The bank was built quite distinctively of two contrasting materials, a core of sand and grit the colour of French mustard overlain with a soft, black, peaty loam. The interior of the circle as defined by the bank was covered with a deposit of mixed subsoil and soil, and once again the subsoil used shows that the material was brought to the site for the purpose and was not from the immediate vicinity.

At some stage in the·complex and contradictory process which cannot be precisely fixed a low, spread, outer bank was added around the outer edge of the almost filled ditch. And as a final stage in the process the whole monument was carefully cloaked in more soil together with stones.

Since the circles are very closely set it was possible to investigate their relationship one to another. In several instances it appeared that one circle had been deliberately set alongside another and physically related to it by one of two means. A second circle added to a first might be appended in the form of a horseshoe to form something like a figure 8 in plan. Alternatively, the outer bank of the secondary circle might be gently overlaid on the outer bank of the other circle. Altogether there were only about a dozen circles, but they are all tightly fitted together.

Why was the group of circles left as it was after a dozen depositions? Where did the people live who came and used the site? Were the deliberate structural relationships between the circles designed to model kinship or other social relationships between the persons whose remains were placed in the circles? All these questions (and many more about the meaning of the extraordinary construction activities which followed each cremation deposition) remain unanswered in spite of the considerable volume of detailed observations made in the course of the excavations.

Rock art in the Jordanian desert.

We are all familiar with graffiti, which many people regard as unsightly vandalism; but we should not think that graffiti are solely a 'modern problem'. In fact the form has a very respectable prehistory, and the study of graffiti through the ages can give us a unique insight into the lives, thoughts and preoccupations of ordinary people, men and women whose private complaints and dreams would never otherwise have a record.

In the Black Desert of eastern Jordan, ancient lava flows have provided particularly tempting smooth and receptive surfaces, and travellers over the ages have accepted the invitation to leave their marks. All sorts of inscriptions occur, reflecting additional light on the other remains found on survey (about which more can be found in the section on landscape and survey).

The earliest carvings were made by prehistoric hunters who operated in the desert some eight thousand years ago. Amongst the elegant sketches of the delicate gazelle which they hunted, they sometimes produced cartoon images of themselves, wearing loose, baggy costumes and carrying their weapons of the hunt. Later, as herders brought their sheep and goats through the region, pastoral themes become common. Hunting, however, continued for a long while. There are strange and unexpected scenes of herds of ostrich, sometimes pursued by men with dogs, and lions hunted by figures on horseback, men who are sometimes shown arrayed in armour and plumed helmets.

By the Roman period the beduin of the area were literate and were able to communicate their ideas and feeling more accurately and precisely in words. A barber with the Roman army complains of the discomfort of his frontier posting. Shepherds record with longing their girlfriends' names, or write insults about their enemies. Nomads draw their favourite camels, or dream of a life away from the dust and the heat of the desert as they carefully engrave imagined scenes of gardens full of flowers, trees and streams of running water.

The coming of Islam is marked by inscriptions of early religious texts, perhaps the pious handiwork of passing pilgrims on their way to Mecca. Some died and found their last resting place in the desert, and

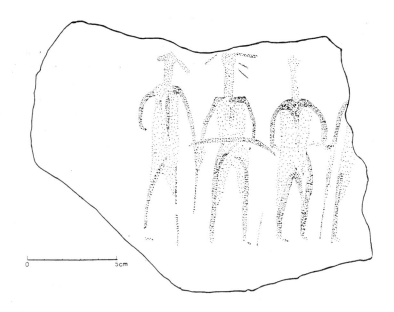

Fig 23. A group of hunters with bows and breeches: Black Desert, Jordan.

their gravestones may give their names and prayers for their souls. Modern inscriptions sill echo age-old themes. There are relatively fresh inscriptions of texts from the Koran, names and dates (the equivalent of 'Kilroy was here'), and representations of the pickup trucks and diesel lorries which are now the 'ships of the desert'.

Ritual and its paraphernalia, Mosphilia, Cyprus

Even man's 'inward and spiritual' beliefs find concrete expression in 'outward and visible signs'. In our own cultural environment we can point to the largest monuments in our historic cities, the great medieval cathedrals, and the smallest symbol of a silver cross worn on a chain, still commonly see. Even in a transcendental religion such as Christianity there is a great many specialised artefacts and a rich world of iconography and symbolism. Archaeologists have long believed intuitively that some of the artefacts found among the remains of extinct societies must similarly be referents to religious beliefs and practices.

In many parts of the Old World a not uncommon find from remote prehistoric contexts has been a small, female figure either carved in stone or modelled in clay. In seeking to define aspects of the world of beliefs to which such female figurines may refer, the archaeologist has almost always been confronted with a major difficulty. Most of these figurines were found in contexts which do not contribute to their interpretation; for example there is a series of tiny, highly stylized, cruciform stone figurines from the west of Cyprus, but most of them have come to museum collections as stray finds, or have been found accompanying a
skeleton in a grave.

A very recent find in Cyprus on the site of Mosphilia (described in the earlier section on settlement) is a very rare example of figurines found associated with what is surely a whole group of objects of cult significance in an interpretable context. In one of the houses at Mosphilia a pit was found, choked with fire-cracked and ochrestained stones and an extraordinary array of 56 assorted objects. The objects included vividly painted pots, unlike those which had been found before in domestic contexts, 19 figurines, some of stone and some of baked clay, a model stool in terracotta, a triton shell, and assorted stone tools of types known from ordinary houses.

Most of the objects were packed in or around the lowest bowl, a great flat-bottomed vessel, which the excavator could immediately recognise as a model of a particular and distinctive type of circular building such as had been excavated at Mosphilia in the previous season. Many of the objects were deliberately mutilated or broken;

Fig 24.   Painted pottery female figure in childbirth. She sits with legs apart on a stool, but her legs and those of the stool have been broken.

the swinging door of the modelled circular building had been wrenched out and the pivotsockets broken; the model had been smeared with yellowish clay. All the circumstances seem to point to the ceremonial breaking, destroying and deposition of a group of objects charged with symbolic power.

Such finality accords with the general picture of what was happening at that time at Mosphilia, for the unique pit had been dug through the last floor level of the last building in the stratified sequence at the site; some time after the deposition in the pit, the the wall of the house collapsed and sealed the pit under its rubble. It appears that the deposition of the group of disfigured objects in the pit was one of the ultimate acts carried out at the settlement as it was being (temporarily) deserted at the end of the 4th millennium B.C.

The pottery figurines are a specially adventurous group of representations. Apart from a single grotesque male figure with protruding, red-bordered eyes and lips, and one animal figure, the figures are female. Almost all have arms outstretched; some are shown standing, and others are seated on stools. The seated female figures have unusually detailed redpainted decoration, and one in particular deserves special attention.

She herself wears a figurine on a necklace. Like the others, this figure has a protruding belly and stumpy, short legs, widely spaced where they join the torso. On the front of the stool, below the belly and between the legs is painted what can only be seen as the head and arms of a baby in the process of being born. Such explicit representations of childbirth are extremely rare, and this is certainly the first from Cyprus. At last there is some unequivocal evidence that some female figurines at least have to do with cult, ritual and ideas of childbirth and fertility.

Section 5: New Directions

To many people it may seem a contradiction that a subject which is devoted to the investigation of the past (the 'back-ward looking curiositie', as a seventeenth century antiquary called it) should also be concerned for the present, and for the future. In fact most archaeologists are deeply involved in relating their work to the present-day world; this aspect of archaeology is the subject of the next section. In this section we look at the ways that archaeologists are looking to the future.

One of the ways in which archaeology remains an exciting subject is the constant development or adoption of new techniques, and the frequent opening of new windows of knowledge. Archaeology is still a very young subject, and the learning curve is therefore still very steep. It is also a practical subject which employs all sorts of equipment for analysis, for survey, for excavation, for recording and data- analysis. So archaeology has been able to profit greatly from the technological revolution of post-war years. Archaeology has always shared interests with all sorts of other disciplines, so that advances in allied disciplines, such as botany, zoology, geography, or soil science, have had their impact in archaeology too through the medium of palaeo-botany or palaeo- environmental research.

Techniques of physical analysis have advanced enormously in the last quarter century, and many of these new methods have proved to have exciting archaeological applications. As one example, obsidian, a black volcanic glass much used in some parts of the world in the same way as flint to make chipped stone tools, can now be characterised and pieces of worked obsidian found on ancient settlements can be identified as having been brought from a particular flow in some zone of volcanic activity which may be hundreds of miles away. Obsidian from lava flows in central Turkey has been identified on settlement sites eight thousand years old in the deep south of Jordan; obsidian from the island of Lipari reached the Italian mainland five thousand years ago; obsidian was exchanged across the United States from the Rockies to the eastern states many centuries before the first European contact.

From the Pieces of the Past

Obsidian is now analysed by the technique of neutron activation analysis, the same technique as is used in the analysis of ceramics described in the section on the investigation of artefacts. The technique is now routine, but only in the mid-1970's it was still at the formative stage and its archaeological applications were experimental. Brand new techniques devised for application in the food industry in the micro-analysis of complex organic substances such as amino-acids and enzymes have recently been successfully applied in archaeology; food residues on or in the surfaces of ancient cooking pots can be identified in terms of these characteristic substances, giving us a quite new and absolutely direct insight into ancient diets. As fast as new and more sophisticated techniques of analysis are devised somewhere some archaeologist will see a potential application.

As with many other subjects archaeology is being revolutionised through the application of computers, and especially micro-computers. Archaeology has uses for computers in every branch of the computer's abilities, number-crunching, database-management, graphics and word-processing. Excavation and survey are notorious for their ability to produce horrifying amounts of routine data, cumbersome to administer, difficult to analyse because of its volume, and extremely expensive to publish for the same reason. For those archaeologists who have had to wrestle hand to hand with the hundred-headed beast of excavation records it will be justification enough of the use of computers if those nimble and tireless machines which do not recognise tedium can take over some of the task. But computer applications must also justify themselves in either of two ways on account of the capital cost of purchasing and running the equipment: in simple terms the applications justify themselves if they enable the archaeologists to produce their end-product more cost-efficiently; and, again, if computer applications allow the archaeologist to extend the reach of the enquiries beyond what could have been managed without their aid.

In terms of the latter of those two justifying features, that of extending archaeological research into new areas which could not otherwise be reached, computers have already shown their worth. In some cases the computational complexity of the statistical dataanalysis which has been applied to certain bodies of archaeological data has been devised only in response to the availability computer power to carry it out; the impracticability of carrying out the computations involved in many of the techniques of multivariate analysis is such that noone would ever have the time to work them through by hand. One can also begin to see a by-product of the availability of computers to sort large bodies of data in complicated ways in that archaeologists can ask quite simple but speculative questions of the data which would not have occurred to them to ask if the volume of data to be sorted in order to obtain the answer would have required several hours or a day or two of manual record-sorting. With a computerised database the archaeologist can ask 'what if ...' type of questions, which the computer can answer readily in a few seconds. In turn the speed with which these speculative questions can be tested means that the archaeologist can develop further questions as he sees how a tentative hypothesis begins to work out.

In terms of cost-effectiveness, it is probably too early to say whether computer applications literally pay off. Certainly they ought to, since the computer can manage text and deal with all kinds of data so much faster than the human archaeologist. There has not yet been a controlled cost-effectiveness test carried out, but common sense says that the computer's clerical efficiencies alone should justify outlay cost. Even in the mundane field of word-processing micro-computers have a particular part to play in archaeological report-writing. What needs to be remembered is that a great deal of archaeological fieldwork is cooperative, and most archaeological final reports on excavation or survey are composed from the pens of several specialists. It is already commonplace for draft versions of parts of the final report to be circulated so that the points of contact (or conflict) between the parts can be identified, the necessary amendments made and the inevitable contradictions resolved. The power of the micro-computer to execute instant, large-scale revisions of the text makes corporate authorship a real possibility since it is never necessary to abandon a laboriously produced typescript and set about retyping a replacement.

Occasionally archaeology makes a new move of its own which is not based on some technical advance or derived from the archaeological application of some new technique from another discipline. Archaeologists have always been adventurers (witness the confrontation of Indiana Jones with the Raiders of the Lost Ark!), but it is not necessary to look to the remoter parts of the globe for space for a new venture. Some new ventures take place in the laboratory, and even within Britain there are dark periods, surprisingly large unexplored areas and novel subjects to be taken up. The world- wide range of human history and prehistory is such a vast subject and one of such enormous variety that most of us are only beginning to be aware that what has been discovered so far is only a very selective scratching of the surface. And wherever the truly innovative archaeologist turns, comfortable old assumptions are toppled and a dramatic and challenging new perspective opens up. A few years ago, for example, there were reports of highly organised irrigation schemes dated to thousands of years B.C. in the Papua New Guinea highlands, when most people had assumed that irrigation was first devised in the already complex societies of Mesopotamia and pre-dynastic Egypt. From a remote part of Thailand came the news of the discovery of evolved bronzeworking at dates millennia earlier than the earliest previously known. And many people will be aware from the newspaper reports of the discoveries of earlier and earlier human ancestors in remote and inaccessible parts of Africa.

It might be thought that it is relatively easy to change the picture of world prehistory by going to work in parts of the world which have been by and large ignored until now. In fact, even in the areas of the world where archaeologists have been working in the field the longest, there have been recent revolutions in our knowledge, and there continue to be new ventures which fly in the face of the received wisdom. Recent work on Rhum, an island in the Inner Hebrides off the west coast of Scotland, has brought to light the earliest evidence human habitation in Scotland, dating back a thousand years and more older than anything previously found. Most archaeologists would not have chosen the Inner Hebrides for such a piece of research, the general expectation being that the isles would constitute something of a retarded periphery.

Similarly, it has always been the·view that, if there had been any very early human occupation of the far north of Britain in the

Pleistocene (Ice Age) period, all trace of it would have been scoured from the landscape by the last phase of major glaciation some twenty to twentyfive thousand years ago. In like vein it has been held that the effects of that last glacial phase would have lasted longer in the Highland massifs, and that groups of hunter-gatherers would have been very slow to return north as the ice retreated. But we have recently learned that palaeolithic hunter-gatherers had returned north of the Arctic Circle in Norway at a remarkably early date. And archaeologists are now searching for cave-sites in the west of Scotland in the hope of learning that the post- glacial re-occupation of Scotland was similarly early.

Along with the fieldwork adventurers and those who perceptively appreciate the potential of bringing together new technical methods of analysis with old archaeological problems we should place the theoretical innovators. It is the commonplace image of the archaeologist to be seen as a rather myopic and naive old figure in tweeds; it is not commonly appreciated outside the subject that archaeology is in fact a rather young discipline whose theoretical formation has only just in the last couple of decades or so reached the threshold of maturity. It is perhaps easier in some respects to engage in theoretical innovation in archaeology than in new ventures of other kinds; it certainly does not require the investment of preparation, teamwork and funds that field exploration demands. It is also perhaps a necessary aspect of theoretical advance that it seems to be a tumult in which competing ideas and contradictory novelties are tossed up and a number are at once shot down or at least regarded with a severe cynicism; among the many initial ballons d'essai, however, when one has the advantage of the perspective of a decade's hindsight, one sees that some contributions have had the quality to withstand the tests and indeed to find themselves incorporated into the establishment of the orthodox.

A new approach to environmental reconstruction

Although we ourselves may live lives in which we are heavily cocooned from the physical environment, people in earlier times were much more in contact with and immediately dependent upon the environmental conditions in which they led their lives. For us, who live in cities of concrete and asphalt, who eat processed foods whose origin as plants and animals may be very remote, who step from heated homes into heated cars or buses, and work in heated offices, it is easy to recognise that we operate in a largely man-made environment. But perhaps it is easier for us now to recognise that we need to be more environmentally aware and sensitive, when we read in our newspapers about the difficulties of farmers facing serious soil erosion, or of the impact on the life in streams and rivers of the drainage of agro-chemicals into the ecosystem. Archaeology has always been concerned to explore the history of the vital and delicate inter-relationship between man and the physical environment.

Traditionally pollen analysis, detailed geomorphology, soil science, and, more recently, the study of snails and other surviving shells in archaeological contexts have been used as climatic and environmental indicators. Diatom analysis has become well-established in fields such as palaeolimnology (the study of ancient lakes), but has been little used in archaeology.

Diatoms are a form of microscopic unicellular algae, living in predominantly aquatic habitats. There are many different kinds of diatom, and they are very specific in their adaptations to the environment; and they are very sensitive to changes in environmental conditions. Diatoms have one other advantage as far as students of the past are concerned, and that is their remains persist in sediments, and can survive for thousands of years. By establishing the particular environmental requirements of contemporary diatom communities it is possible to use the identification of the microscopic diatom remains from ancient sediments to infer the conditions under which the sediments formed. Diatom analysis has been used in the study of sea-level change, for example, and changes in the nature and direction of ancient water-courses.

Like other methods of discerning aspects of past physical environments within which human communities have lived, diatom analysis is therefore capable of offering clues to the nature of the

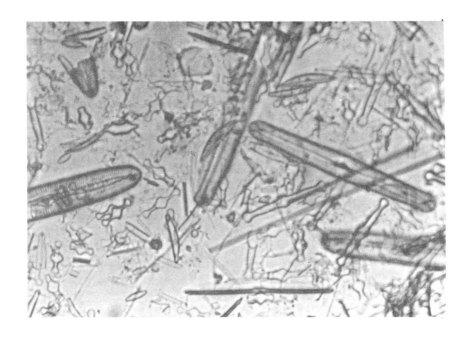

Fig 25. *The microscope slide is filled with diatoms of many different species.*

environment, and to changes in that environment over time. Research which is currently in progress, however, encourages the expectation that diatom analysis will become a useful tool in the exploration and explanation of more specifically archaeological deposits, such the ubiquitous but mysterious pits, ditches and their fills which are found on so many archaeological sites. Diatom analysis may be able to help in understanding how the fill of a pit was formed, or how a ditch became silted, and also something of the nature of the very local, man-affected environment of the settlement at that time.

In recent years work has also begun on assessing the potential of
In recent years work has also begun on assessing the potential of diatom analysis as a means of sourcing the clays used by ancient potters. In this situation the diatoms in the clays relate to the time of the geological formation of the clay beds, and the assumption is that different clays, laid down at various times in different places, will

contain somewhat different diatom populations. Diatoms can be be detected in the fired clay of ancient potsherds, and it should therefore be possible at least to discern within a group of pots which look superficially the same that different clay sources have been used, and therefore that pottery from more than one source is present. The hope is that it may prove to be possible to 'finger-print' particular clay sources and thus to relate archaeological finds of pottery to the place of manufacture.

The research on the archaeological applications of diatom analysis is still in progress. Some applications already look highly likely to become standard (for example, the definition of the environmental conditions of ancient waterside settlements such as those at Eskmeals in Cumbria, referred to above). Other applications are still very much in the early and experimental stages. But the general indications are enough to encourage optimism that diatom analysis will one day have many, diverse and highly informative applications in archaeology.

Ed-Dur, United Arab Emirates.

Much archaeological interest over the last century in the Middle East has been concentrated on centres like Babylonia in S. Iraq, the Bible lands, and pharaonic Egypt. For a variety of reasons it has taken a long time for interest to develop in the important historical role played by the peoples of the Arabian peninsula and the Gulf. As the states in that region have become more concerned about their own national archaeological heritage in the last two decades or so, very exciting discoveries have been reported relating to ancient cultures and civilizations dating back thousands of years before the birth of Islam. Taking up once more the image of the jigsaw puzzle, however, we have as yet found and turned over only a very few of the pieces in a very large and panoramic picture.

Ed-Dur is the site of a large, ancient city on the shores of the Gulf in the United Arab Emirates. The surface finds include an impressive proportion of imported goods, such as glazed Parthian pottery and pottery and millefiori glass from the eastern Roman Empire. Our interest in such a site (4 km by 1 km in approximate extent) can only be increased when we recognise the interest of the Romans of that time in the thriving trade which linked Egypt, Mesopotamia and the east Mediterranean with 'Arabia Felix', India and even the Far East.

In October 1986 an invitation from the Emirate of Umm al Qawain was given to an international quartet of archaeologists to undertake a feasibility study of the site in cooperation with the government of Umm al Qawain. On the basis of the first exploratory season of work a programme has now been planned for a three-year large-scale investigation of the site. The project links with the government of Umm al Qawain the four universities of Copenhagen, Ghent, Lyon and Edinburgh, and its international composition and carefully planned dovetailing of interests shows how archaeology is changing and developing towards new ways of working.

Archaeologists have long been accustomed to working in teams for fieldwork projects, and to working as part of a multi-disciplinary attack on a particular problem. But this welding of teams together into a higher level of integrated research is still quite novel. Part of the purpose is simply economic and another part is practical. To tackle the archaeology of such a huge site with a view to understanding something of its functioning and history is completely beyond the resources of any archaeological researcher. And for one director to tackle so complex a question single-handed would require a thoroughly unrealistic programme of field research lasting for decades.

In the first season each of the four cooperators undertook a different aspect of the initial assessment of the site. The Danish team worked near the centre of the site, and found an area of substantial, stone-built domestic structures. Among their finds were beautiful imported pieces of technically advanced and luxurious Roman glass, probably made in W. Syria. Working on the coastward side of the site, the French team also found themselves in an area of impressive, large houses. One of the houses contained two larger than life-size stone statues of standing eagles, whose closest stylistic parallels occur far away in north Iraq, at Hatra, the remarkable capital of a Parthian desert kingdom.

Next into the field came the British team, who worked on the inland side of the site. They also undertook the preliminary survey of an area south of the main site, where surface pottery suggested the remains of a much earlier settlement dating to before 2000 B.C. In their main excavation they located an area within the cemetery of the city. The tombs had almost all been despoiled in antiquity, but there was still plenty of material left to enable the archaeologists to assess the date and quality of the cemetery. The tombs themselves varied in size, sophistication and quality. Each consisted of a stone-lined chamber cut into the ground. The simplest tombs were an oval pit lined with a drystone retaining wall. The larger tombs consisted of a rectangular chamber with walls nearly two metres high and a paved stone floor. The chamber was approached by a stepped passage, and would probably was originally roofed with a stone vault. Among the finds iron weapons, beads, a bronze animal head and numerous decorative bone inlays, and of course a great deal of pottery.

The site is clearly that of an important city which was in contact with the world of Mesopotamia as well as the Mediterranean coastlands which were part of the Hellenistic- Roman world. Its situation on a sheltered bay which would have provided an excellent harbour points surely to the city's role as an intermediary point on the important long distance trade route to the Indian Ocean. The prospects are exciting, but the realisation of this particular part of the jigsaw puzzle of history lies in the future.

Data-capture and on-site computerised fieldwork records

Archaeologists have found computers, and especially micro-computers, very adaptable to their purposes. A number of archaeologists are now seeking to extend the use of portable computers into archaeological fieldwork. The work is still at the experimental stage. Different groups are trying out different manufacturer's products, and are writing their own software. At present there are few fully operational, proven systems, and no standardisation.

The logic of taking battery-powered machines into the field is that, if computers are to be used for the management of data from archaeological fieldwork, it is more efficient to employ them for the primary recording of the data. To write the information on forms and in notebooks by hand, and then to transcribe it at a later date is not only less efficient but also opens the possibility of incorporating errors during the copying process. If the archaeologist is working at a distance from his permanent base, and his computer is kept at that base, then he is losing the opportunity to analyse his new field information in any sophisticated way until the fieldwork is over and the possibility of interaction and feedback is missed.

In the wake of the micro-computer came the portable computer, and the hand-held computer. These are battery-powered machines which can be operated wherever the user happens to be, and without the need for a stable electricity supply. The so-called laptop computers were designed for the mobile executive, who might wish to continue his work while away from his desk, but they are particularly well suited also to the environment of archaeological fieldwork. Portable computers are as powerful as the ordinary desktop office machines, and they allow the archaeologist to take computer power for the storage and analysis of the masses of collected field data much closer to the scene of the fieldwork.

The hand-held computer is not confined to the site-hut; it can go right into the trench to the point where the find is made and first recorded, or across the landscape in the pocket of the field-surveyor. It becomes an electronic notebook, taking in the information as it is observed, holding it in orderly fashion, and copying it to its parent computer whenever required. The computer recording can thus be taken to the point of discovery and first recording, and it therefore never needs to be copy-typed from one record to another because the hand- held computer can transfer data electronically.

A major concern of the field director is always the security of the fieldwork records; paper records are vulnerable in the field, without considering the dangers of incorrect or incomplete recording of the information in the notebook in the first place. The software for the hand-held or portable computer can be written to insure as far as possible against forgetting to put in some of the data, or trying to put in incorrect data. The computer has the ability to duplicate the vital data it holds onto other media, thereby providing the means of protection which the field archaeologist needs.

A major fieldwork season on a large project is nowadays costed in tens of thousands of pounds. While fieldwork costs increase, the prices of micro-computer equipment decrease year by year in real terms. At the time of writing a hand-held computer can be bought for under £100, and a powerful portable, as capable as a desk-top office model, for under £1000. Increased efficiency in data-recording and improvements in dataanalysis during and after the fieldwork on the route to publication can represent the saving of considerable sums of money. As far as the fieldworking archaeologist is concerned, the computer may soon begin to be seen as an essential tool that is not to be left in the office when the real work gets under way.

New directions in archaeological research publication

Archaeologists have a responsibility to publish the results of their investigations, just like other scientists.
What was formerly thought to be 'full' publication is now thought insufficient in its detail to support the investigations of the next generation of research students. Standards of what constitutes 'full publication' have changed.

At the same time there are other, pressing economic factors which require field-archaeologists to look for new and more efficient ways to disseminate their findings. Major excavation reports may now sell at more than £100 per volume, and many excavations require several volumes to encompass the huge quantities of data and analysis. The bodies which publish the established learned journals are finding that their escalating printing bills cannot be matched by pro rata increases in the subscription prices; and other means must be found to contain the cost of scientific publication.

On the other hand we have recent technological innovations which can be of service. These allow us to economise on the cost of publication and at the same time facilitate the preparation and publication of more detailed reports. Archaeologists have been quick to exploit the potential of microfiche for the condensation of printed material and its reproduction at low cost. They are also seeking to take advantage of the micro-computer's ability to generate camera- ready copy for the printer in order to publish more quickly and more cheaply. And only just over the horizon is the prospect of large databases of archaeological research material being 'published' by being made accessible over computer networks.

The production of copy for publication from first tentative draft to camera-ready copy can be one process, controlled throughout by the author. In the case of the report on archaeological fieldwork the task of collaborative authorship under the guidance of the director is particularly well adapted to word-processing on micro- computers. Archaeologists are becoming quite accustomed to producing their own copy, ready for the printer, saving both time and money. No-one can claim that the printed end-results are the most handsome examples of the publisher's art; but some loss of aesthetic quality is a small price to pay for having books which are quicker coming to press and can be afforded by more readers and more libraries.

The major national agencies in the world of archaeology, and their counterparts at regional and local level, are working at transferring the vast amounts of data of which they are the custodians onto computerised database management systems. Large museum collections, the lists of scheduled ancient monuments (in British legal parlance the state-protected archaeological sites of national importance), the gazeteers of sites and buildings of archaeological and historical interest, the National Monuments Record, all are in the process of transfer. Once the databases are made accessible to remote users from their own computer terminals, it will become possible for the user to obtain for himself the information he wants. Already there are computerised archives of individual recent excavations, making the information available for consultation in exactly the same way as it was recorded and used by those who carried out the excavation and produced the published report.

The pace of the electronic information revolution is so fast that 'tomorrow's world' quickly becomes reality, and often as quickly becomes obsolete. Already companies are marketing the whole of the world's most famous encyclopaedia held on a single compact disc, to be consulted through the medium of a personal computer. Perhaps the microfiche, which a number of archaeologists have found discomforting and inconvenient, will prove to have a short life, soon supplanted by electronic dissemination of networked information or digital audio tapes.

Section 6: Public issues

The past is not remote, not even when it is distant in time from our own time. A novelist began one of his novels with the attractive and memorable declaration that 'the past is a foreign country'. But for many of us that is not so, because it is our past, and we feel close to it, even part of it in the sense of being its present product. We feel a need to recognise our cultural roots, and in particular to see something of those roots in the physical cultural heritage of our country, in our museums and in our countryside. In our towns and cities we are always aware of the historical environment in which we live and work, whether in the antique form of an inspiring landmark such as a cathedral or in the more prosaic and less ancient form of a pothole caused by a collapsing 19th century sewer. Our environment is just as much historical and manmade when we look at the rural landscape, although many people seem to regard the countryside as purely a natural environment of plants, animals, soils, geology and climate. Archaeology enables us to recognize, investigate, interpret and conserve that historical and cultural landscape, whether in the context of a major city with early medieval origins or in a wild, romantic and superficially uninhabited such as the far north of Scotland.

Archaeology is not a form of escapism. For everyone interested in seeking to unravel the story of the past, archaeological investigation, whether involving adventurous fieldwork in some remote or romantic part of the world or the vicarious pleasure of exploring the library shelves, archaeology may give a great deal of private enjoyment. However, everyone with an active interest in the physical remains of our past will encounter the extensive public interface of the subject. Most of the professional archaeologists (that is, those who earn their living through being archaeologists) are in some form of public employment; they may work in museums, in the planning department of the local authority, in a university, or in one of several government agencies concerned, and they will be constantly aware that their jobs are concerned with the public, the state, the national heritage, or the community.

If we recognise that we share a common heritage from our

forebears, we must also accept that we have a shared duty in our turn to hand on that inheritance. Here there is a serious problem for our generation, one which is felt more keenly by some than others. Many aspects of our present way of life must seriously damage parts of our cultural and historical heritage. The obvious conflicts, such as the replacement of parts of our older city-centres by modern shopping and commercial developments, are not the only ones. The spread of housing, the building of new factory-estates, the extraction of minerals, and even the development of more heavily mechanised agriculture, all risk destroying some previously unknown or unexplored fragments of the historical landscape. One of the obstacles to the recognition of this constant threat and erosion of the physical heritage is that of ignorance: it is easy to feel that the major historical buildings which we can see in the centre of our town should be conserved, but it is much harder to take steps to preserve a heritage in the landscape which largely lies invisible below the soil and which is not yet even identified and catalogued.

Clearly not all remains of the past are equally important, and obviously not all can be conserved, or are worth conserving. But there is a need to try to rescue some record of the past and some information from a site which must be destroyed. The dilemma is often that, in the present state of our understanding of the past, we are unable to assess whether an archaeological site can be safely sacrificed without investigation of any kind. Rescue archaeology has become an important feature of the lives of many archaeologists in recent years. For many professional archaeologists rescue archaeology is their means of earning a livelihood. For university archaeologists and archaeology students it has become a means whereby research can be carried out, experience can be gained, and an important public service can be performed. Much of our programme of excavations in Britain over the last twenty years has been rescue excavation carried out in cooperation with and funded by the government authorities responsible for the care of our heritage.

More recently we have added rescue survey work to the repertoire. It may come as surprise to some people that in this country, where archaeology has been most actively pursued for longer than almost any other country, we still do not have a simple, primary record of the visible sites in the landscape. Where marginal land is brought into cultivation under government or EEC incentive grants, it is often found that our perception of the land as marginal is a narrow one, and that the land was formerly intensively used. Modern arable farming will remove for ever those surface traces of more ancient farming and settlement landscapes. Similarly with the even more rapid turn to forestry, for which there are again cash incentives. In those parts of Scotland which are not economic under contemporary agricultural methods vast tracts of land which have been inhabited from time immemorial until the Highland clearances are being submerged under conifercrops. And since they have never known modern, mechanised farming, these same areas are often full of the richest archaeological and historical remains. Under modern archaeological surveying techniques whole landscapes can be mapped. And if the mapping is not done at once, the forestry plough will rip the evidence to shreds and the roots of a blanket of forest trees will complete the work of elimination.

Rescue, or salvage archaeology, the casualty department of the archaeological hospital service, is not confined to the developed western world. Development of different kinds, and often on a quite massive scale, is pursued in many other countries. For example the great rivers of the Near East, the Nile, the Tigris and the Euphrates, have been dammed and huge inland seas are being created which drown several hundred known archaeological sites at only three to five years notice. Vast irrigation schemes may follow which will severely damage the historical landscape over hundreds of square kilometres. And today's archaeologists from countries like ours are playing an important role in international rescue surveys and excavations in many of the countries of the developing world.

Archaeologists also have an important role to play in interpreting the past for a wider public. At a very simple level, it is often said that, since most archaeological research is carried out at the public expense, largely through the medium of rescue or salvage work, the archaeologists have a duty to inform the public if they are to give 'value for money'. In some cases this simple relationship may exist, for example where the archaeologists have been employed to investigate a monument or an area of historical landscape in order to increase the understanding of it and provide a better and more satisfying interpretation of it to the visiting public.

There is, however, a deeper level of responsibility to the public, akin to that felt by many scientists (in the broad sense of that word). The knowledge and understanding of human societies which the archaeologist can win needs to be shared: while any of us may enjoy the private right to enjoy aspects of our history and heritage, when new information and some fresh understanding has been won at the expense of the investigation of some part of our archaeological heritage none of us has the right to regard that as private. Scientists acknowledge an obligation to make their findings public, in other words to publish. In the first instance most archaeologists recognise that obligation to publish in terms of the production of a full' report of their work, aimed at the community of (interested) fellow-archaeologists. In a wider sense there is also an obligation to publish some briefer synthesis of the results for a broader community of archaeological interest. And in a wider sense again there is the obligation to publish some account of the archaeologists' understanding of the human past in a form which is meaningful to all aspects of the general public. There is a need for books of every kind from those suitable for children at primary school, through those expensive 'coffee-table' heavy-weights, that important midway market of public libraries, sophisticated school student, junior university student and committed private purchaser, to the 'popular' paper-back, the newspaper article, and even the glossy 'in-flight' magazine. But in these days of multiple communication media, publication means more than producing printed material for all the diverse sectors of a literate public; an important medium of the popularisation of many sciences, including archaeology and history (popularisation in the sense of reaching a very broad public) has been the television documentary, and paralleling the printed popular archaeology magazines there is now an established BBC radio magazine devoted to the subject.

Finally, and coming full circle in this book, there is another, though narrower, aspect to the question of archaeology and the wider, public world; and that is the place of the archaeology in the world of scholarship. The University of Edinburgh declared its belief that archaeology was a discipline in its own right, and one suitable for general study by undergraduate students, by appointing a professor to profess and teach the subject from October

From the Pieces of the Past

1927, an anniversary celebrated by the exhibition which occasioned this book. Archaeology had been accepted as an academic discipline within the scientific community earlier than 1927 in only a very few places, notably in Denmark. And it has become more common since that date in British universities, even making its appearance as an examinable school subject in a small minority of British schools. Nevertheless, there has been (and continues to be) a degree of controversy as to whether archaeology is an independent discipline on a par with, for example history, biology or physics.

The situation of archaeology in the community of scientific disciplines has not been made easier to resolve by the difficulty which exists in fitting it within any of the convenient categories whereby western traditions compartmentalize knowledge. Archaeology is certainly concerned with the human past, like history; but it treats of that subject through the medium of physical artefacts, which can be analysed, measured and counted; it must also be recognised that archaeology, in company with the social sciences such as anthropology and sociology, looks at man in society; and it is also concerned with human communities in their spatial relation to each other and the physical environment, thus having much in common with geography.

A quarter of a century ago a few young archaeologists in Britain and the United States of America began to assert vociferously the independence and uniqueness of the discipline of archaeology. Their difficult language and their lack of respect (indeed their contempt) for the work of their predecessors (including their own teachers in many cases) combined with the radical ideas which they proposed to ensure that their revolutionary programme for New Archaeology was greeted with raised blood pressure, low levels of comprehension and general antipathy. Perhaps time has conspired to make their revolution seem simple common sense, or possibly there has been a convergence whereby archaeology is beginning to find itself in tune with certain contemporary cultural and philosophical views.

At the core of the New Archaeology's programme was a concept of human culture in which artefacts, the things made and used by man, are to be understood as relating to every aspect of the shared belief and behaviour systems which we call culture. Previously

143

archaeologists had considered artefacts as technical products whose simple functions as knives or houses could be ascertained; the new theory said that a simple knife might simultaneously relate to a rich variety of different aspects, economic, technical, overtones of social status, symbolic perhaps in its wearing. For archaeologists the message was that through the medium of its artefacts we might have access to even the most abstract aspects of ideology, meaning and symbolism. Now, such views of the cultural semiology of objects have become the common currency of philosophers and sociologists.

To believe that we have the potential to reach every complex aspect of the cultural patterns of an extinct community via the broken, corroded fragments of its artefacts requires a degree of optimism which is often difficult to sustain in the face of archaeological reality. On the other hand nothing worth knowing is easily discovered, and the great advances in human knowledge and understanding have been slow in coming to fruition: archaeology is still a very young discipline which has yet to develop through to full maturity. The learning curve is still very steep in archaeology. This can be observed by comparing any two textbooks covering the same area or aspect of the subject which were published a generation apart; in archaeology textbooks are outdated often before they are published because of new discoveries in the field, a completely new light shed on subjects by fresh research, or new developments in our techniques of investigation. It is no contradiction to predict that, at such a rate of development, we may confidently expect that the further we move into the future the better we shall be able to see into the past.

Caithness marginal land survey, Highland Region, Scotland

Land utilisation in Britain has generally been intensive over a period of many centuries. And large-scale changes in land use, with consequent erasure of the physical traces of earlier patterns of settlement and land use, are no new phenomenon in our history. Today the pace and scale of change, for example the encouragement of massive afforestation programmes, pose serious problems: as well as concern for the effect on local communities, there has to be a care for the environment, and for the historical aspect of the landscape as containing a unique record of the past.

This last aspect is a particular concern of the archaeologists. They would not wish to see the erasure of the past from the landscape without at least some attempt at salvaging as complete a record as is possible of the remains which are to disappear. And yet they often find themselves in a very difficult position when confronted with development plans for wholesale change. It is difficult to make a case for the importance of undertaking a survey to record the remains in an area which most people think of as of little use to humans except for forestry, especially when the information which one suspects will show that those areas were formerly much more intensively populated and used has yet to be documented. Without some grasp of the generality of the surviving remains in an area it is also difficult to advise on what choice fragments within a landscape should be marked out for preservation as part of the cultural heritage. The speed at which redevelopment programmes can be implemented also embarrasses the archaeologists, who can rarely deploy corresponding resources to interpose a primary archaeological survey in the brief time available.

Cooperation between the relevant government agencies and the Edinburgh University Archaeology Department has been aimed at forestalling the worst of these possible scenarios in the face of large-scale afforestation and other development programmes in what is today thought of as marginal land in Caithness, the north-easternmost county of the Scottish mainland. With the help of funding from these government agencies, teams of student surveyors have covered more than 500 square kilometres of land that had previously received only relatively superficial and very uneven archaeological attention. One of the major logistical problems of survey work, the length of time it takes to quarter the ground, has been reduced in magnitude by putting as many as seven teams of surveyors at a time into the landscape. Another logistical problem is less susceptible, however: there is only a very narrow 'window' in the year when survey work is practicable, when the worst of the winter weather is past, and before the vegetation begins to grow again, obscuring the slight undulations and irregularities which may betray the remains of former occupation and land use.

At this stage in the work it is too early to say with any authority what results the research will produce. The survey data, even in its present undigested form, is nevertheless replete with new insights, new kinds of monument, and fresh light on aspects of Caithness history. A few instances may help to indicate the unexpected strengths of the survey data, as well as illustrating how the survey calibrates the alarming rate of damage and erosion which this century has wrought.

The long cairns of Caithness, dating, as we now think, to between 3000 and 2500 B.C., have long been known, and several have been investigated. For those which have been long known we now have detailed plans of their surface details, and new cairns have been added to the list. The cairns have been shown by excavation to be the final product of a long and complex architectural development, and the surveyors have been able to record similar indications on a number of the other mounds. Their work on those cairns which were already fairly well surveyed also documents the alarming and measurable progress of erosion and damage which many are suffering. Dating a little later than the cairns, perhaps about 2500 – 1500 B.C., are the arrays of stone rows, otherwise unknown in Britain. One of these monuments is in the guardianship of the state, but another, at Upper Dounreay, which was known and recorded in 1911, has been severely and massively damaged in the intervening 75 years.

As a result of the survey more than half of the known brochs of Caithness, those circular, tower-like houses of some 2000 years ago, are now surveyed and planned in detail. Few indeed have been excavated, and only one to modern standards, which means that the measured surface detail of such a large sample is particularly valuable. In the light of information from brochs elsewhere which have been excavated it is possible to analyse how a number of the Caithness brochs developed in architectural terms, and even to see their possible antecedents in earlier architectural forms. Another defensive type of structure is the 'cliff castles' with which the coast of

146

Caithness is liberally dotted. This almost completely uninvestigated class of monuments is in danger of keeping its secrets for ever, for heavy coastal erosion is removing them at a measurable rate. During the decade of the survey programme it has been possible to monitor the quite alarming rate at which they are being diminished.

Fig 26. Part of the elevation of an abandoned long-house farm building.

In the decay wrought by time and in the face of the imminent threat of destruction by changing land use there is at least a degree of social equality. Extensive stretches of a bygone agricultural landscape have been mapped. These represent the plots, fields, farmyards and farm buildings from which the population went during the traumatic period of the clearances of the early 19th century, an agricultural pattern of unknown antiquity. Amongst these remains are also the decaying ruins of the large houses of the lairds and the owners of the great estates.

At the time of writing the projected survey programme is almost complete, and by far the greater part of the marginal land in the county of Caithness has been covered. The work has put on record a bewildering variety of remains, ranging in date from about 3000 B.C. to the near present, and amounting to more than 6000 entries in the cumulative catalogue. It is as well that the work was started when it was, for in the meanwhile substantial areas of surveyed land have been ripped by the forestry ploughs and are now under trees. The survey has already provided an index against which informed decisions can be made as to which sites must be preserved if at all possible, which would repay further investigation before forestry removes them, and which can be allowed to disappear, with at least some basic record of their existence and form having been made. At the same time the survey is also providing a sound foundation of data for research into the history and prehistory of Caithness settlement and land-use.

Eski Mosul Dam Salvage Archaeology Project: rescue in N. Iraq

The need to investigate and record the information in archaeological sites which are to disappear in the course of necessary redevelopment is not a concern restricted to the countries of the western world. Large-scale salvage archaeology projects have been going on in the Near East, for example, since UNESCO co-ordinated international archaeological help to rescue the ancient temples and other sites behind the Aswan High Dam in Upper Egypt. Further huge dams have been built or are under construction not only on the other great rivers of the Near East, the Tigris and the Euphrates, but also on their tributaries.

The dam on the Euphrates just north of the town of Eski Mosul in the far north-west of Iraq serves as an illustration of the sudden threat of the elimination of many archaeological sites of all periods and the archaeological response. The scale of the archaeological problem is magnified by the size of the manmade lake behind the dam, the density of historical occupation in the river valley, and the speed with which such a vast civil engineering enterprise moves from its public inception to the completion of construction and then to the filling of the lake behind the dam.

The area to be drowned had been surveyed by Iraqi archaeologists, and an estimated 150 settlement sites were known to be condemned. These sites ranged in size from small villages through sizeable towns to small cities, some of which had been in continuous occupation over several millennia. The area was known to be of historical importance, being the northern (and completely unknown and unexplored) part of ancient Assyria, and to have been one of the key routes up the Euphrates into what is now S. E. Turkey. The extent of the proposed lake was that of an inland sea, reaching back up the valley almost to the Turkish frontier and stretching up to 30 kilometres across the valley. The time available was only from 1982 until 1986, when the dam would be completed and the lake would start to form.

The Directorate-General of Antiquities for Iraq threw in all the resources that they could find, and invited foreign missions to join them. The British response was organised under the umbrella of the British Archaeological Expedition in Iraq. Expedition staff resident in

Iraq undertook the brunt of the work, and teams from institutions such as Edinburgh and Manchester Universities and the British Museum came in on a rota to share the use of vehicles, equipment and the field headquarters. By 1986 British teams had investigated a total of twenty archaeological sites, and almost all the known sites in the valley had been at least tested. Some sites were chosen for larger-scale investigation and excavated over two or three years. In 1985 the waters behind the dam began to rise as the engineers undertook the last stages of construction, and by the spring of 1986 most of the valley was drowned. Edinburgh University had the privilege of excavating on the last site to be dug within site of the Syrian and Turkish frontiers at the very top end of the lake, while the waters of the lake rose day by day towards their site.

It will be some years yet before all the work which was done in those hectic seasons has been processed, published and the results digested. But it is nevertheless easy to assess the general value of the exercise. Each site investigated will have produced grist to the mills of research, and many of the participating teams will be grateful for the opportunities to obtain bodies of new research material. Of broader interest, however, thanks to the dam project, a great deal of research has been concentrated in one area which was previously practically a blank on any archaeological map. One of the major profits to be derived will be seen in the ability to relate many different sites of any period to one another. Usually archaeologists have chosen the sites of their excavations without regard to their wider context within the network of other settlements and their communications networks.

In schemes like the Saddam Dam project we now have enough information about most periods to be able to see something of the broad ebb and flow of history within an area in terms of all the settlements rather than by extrapolation from a single site. Clearly the settlement history of the area contains periods of very high density of settlement and other periods when the area was only thinly populated.

The four sites on which Edinburgh University teams were involved each provided their research pay-off in different forms, and they can serve as typical of the rest. At Kharabeh Shattani, where there were two seasons of excavation, three short periods of occupation were stratified on the one site. The earliest occupation was found only at the last moment and very limited amounts of information were recovered. The second period of occupation, at some time in the early 5th millennium B.C., has produced research material from a widespread N. Mesopotamian culture of precocious complexity of economic organisation. The craft industry and sophisticated distribution of its ceramics are the subject of the investigation by neutron activation analysis illustrated elsewhere in this book. The last period of occupation at Kharabeh Shattani was late in the first millennium B.C., after the fall of the Assyrian Empire, and in what has been for modern scholars an historical and archaeological Dark Age. Suddenly the Saddam Dam project has produced a series of sites of this previously undocumented period, and they will form the archaeological foundation of our understanding of life in Assyria in the decades and centuries immediately after the collapse of the political and administrative superstructure of the Assyrian kingdom.

While digging at Kharabeh Shattani, the Edinburgh team also dug a sounding under the modern village, where evidence of the earlier occupation of the site in later Sassanian times was found. The attractive stamped pottery is being put together with that from all the other sites of the period in the area in a study which is identifying individual stamps; by means of the geographical distribution of the stamps it will be possible to gain some understanding of the nature of the economic infrastructure of the period in terms of the centralisation or localisation of the pottery industry.

Another site, looking extraordinarily like the remains of a clearance settlement in the highlands of Scotland, was surveyed and drawn by members of the Edinburgh team, and later shown by another British team to be the remains of a medieval Islamic hamlet. The final Edinburgh excavation, at a site called Shelgiya, was the narrow investigation of one period of occupation on a multi-period settlement. Shelgiya had been assessed with a surface survey and sounding trenches by another British team, and it was then decided to concentrate on obtaining a sample of the changing material culture of one particular period, the fourth millennium B.C., the formative period for urbanism, which was well represented there but very poorly known in general in N. Mesopotamia.

Working in such salvage archaeology projects, the archaeologists need to take a short-term, opportunist view. They have no choice as to the area, and little chance to think in terms of long-term or large-scale excavation programmes. The results of each individual investigation may be small, sometimes apparently miniscule. But the sum total of the work of all the teams involved adds up to an interlocking patch of jigsaw puzzle pieces.

Upper Plym Valley Survey, Dartmoor National Park, Devon

There are many parts of Britain where historically recent depopulation and the absence of modern, intensive land-use have allowed the survival of the fossilised remains of older systems of land-use. In some areas these priceless historic landscapes are currently under threat of destruction, for example, from extractive industries or forestry.

Dartmoor in the south-west of England is in the special position of being a National Park. Many of its millions of annual visitors go there to appreciate the spacious grandeur of the scenery and the natural beauty of a great wild place. In fact Dartmoor preserves abundant traces of 4000 years of very varied and often intensive human use. When the Upper Plym Valley in the south-western part of Dartmoor was acquired by the National Trust and taken into guardianship on account of its known archaeological wealth by the English Historic Buildings and Monuments Commission, it was decided to use the area to provide greater public access and to take the opportunity to offer to the public an interpretation of the valley in terms of its long history of occupation and land-use.

The intensive survey and recording of the Upper Plym Valley was carried out between 1982 and 1986 in order to build a full database of the surviving physical remains as a foundation for the production of interpretative material for visitors. In the course of mapping the whole area of 25 square kilometres at a scale of 1:1000, the groups of student-surveyors recorded nearly 2000 individual monuments, 550 of these requiring planning at a larger scale. Part of the process of assembling and assessing all the information was the scrutiny of available aerial photographs and, of course, a search among the various documentary sources for useful references.

Agricultural landscapes

Between three and four thousand years ago most of Dartmoor was intensively farmed and relatively densely inhabited, and in the Upper Plym Valley there are to be seen the surprisingly well-preserved and extensive remains relating to all aspects of the life of these Bronze Age communities. The broad landscape was divided by far-reaching stone walls, known locally as reaves, which served as major territorial boundaries. Sometimes the smaller scale reduction of the landscape

153

Fig 27. *The river runs past remains of tin-streaming; beyond the river medieval pillow mounds for rabbit warrening are scattered across the remains of a prehistoric settlement.*

into fields can also be recognised. The settlement pattern of the inhabitants of the valley are to be seen in the form of little clusters of round, stone-built houses, usually set within a stone enclosing wall. These typical enclosed settlements have been recognised as ancient by the local people of recent times, who call them 'pounds', but no-one had suspected until recent excavations elsewhere on the moor that they represented settlement of a period more than three thousand years ago. As well as their villages and farmsteads, their fields and the wider territorial divisions, survey reveals their places of burial in cists and cairns, and the stone circles and stone rows which they or their predecessors erected.

Superimposed on this practically complete prehistoric landscape there are widespread remains of a medieval agricultural landscape. The longhouses are thoroughly recognisable, and sometimes their associated fields and even the signs of their cultivation can be traced. From medieval times, however, the moor became the scene of two important and very dissimilar industries, the warrening of rabbits and the mining of tin, both of which have left their distinctive marks on the landscape for those who have eyes to see.

Rabbit warrening

The warrening of rabbits was an important economic activity in former times, its purpose being to provide both meat and fur. The job of the warrener was to manage an enclosed area prepared and maintained for the commercial exploitation of rabbits. The earliest documented reference to rabbit meat is its 13th century appearance on the menu of royal feasts. It seems that the rabbit was a deliberate introduction to Britain from mainland Europe at some time after the Norman Conquest in the 11th century, and it is probable that warrening was brought in either by the royal court or by the monasteries with their strong connections with France. Until recent times rabbit meat remained an important element in the diet at various social levels, not least because rabbit provided a source of fresh meat through the winter at times when the over-wintering of farm livestock was impracticable. Rabbit fur was valued as both a lining and a trimming for garments, but by the 19th century it was mostly used in the manufacture of felt hats.

In the Upper Plym Valley the physical remains and the documentary sources attest the presence of five separate warrens. Of these, Trowlesworthy warren may have originated in the original 12th century importation of the industry. Ditsworthy dates at least to the 17th century, and by the 19th century it incorporated Legis Tor warren, also on the N. bank, and Hentor and Willings Walls warrens on the S. bank of the river.

The warrener was of course concerned to contain his rabbit population and not to allow them to escape into the countryside; in view of their ability to wreak depradation on the crops local farmers shared the warrener's concern for containment. At Trowlesworthy a water barrier was found to be sufficient for this purpose, and the 12th century lease names the River Plym and its tributaries as the boundaries of the land granted to Sampson de Traylysworthy by Baldwin de Redvers at an annual rent of four shillings. The 1807 lease of Hentor and Willings Walls warrens on the S. bank of the river records them as being open to the moor on the E. side.

The western and northern sides of the Legis Tor warren were defined by a barrier impenetrable to rabbits. Coursed masonry revets the inner side of a substantial earthen bank. The vertical wall face prevents the rabbits from scaling the bank, while the absence of a view across the wall deters them from burrowing. The N.E. limit of the Ditsworthy warren seems to have been marked by a low earthen bank topped with wooden palings.

Within the areas of warrening the largest proportion of remains consists of 'pillow mounds' or 'buries'. These sub- rectangular earthen constructions, mostly about 20 to 30 metres long and from 6 to 8 metres broad, are up to 1 metre high, and are clearly to be seen both on the ground and from the air. They were constructed to provide a suitable habitat for burrowing, and were apparently built on a stone foundation to aid drainage and with a drainage ditch around the mound. A total of 193 pillow mounds has been recorded from the warrens in the valley.

A third and vital element in the warrener's work was the control of predators such as stoats, weasels and, in former times, polecats. The Dartmoor warreners adapted the traditional vermin traps by using a good deal of stone where others used wood; the dressed stone, however, has mostly been taken for reuse elsewhere when the warrening ceased and the traps were abandoned. The most important element was in the siting of the traps on animal routeways, and funnel walls were constructed, sometimes X-shaped and sometimes Y-shaped in plan, to direct the animal into the trap. Traces of only 5 traps were recorded, though funnel walls indicate the former presence of at least another 48 traps set strategically round the pillow mound complexes.

Tin mining

Since man discovered the value of tin as an alloying ingredient to mix with copper to make bronze, tin has been a strategically important metal, its significance enhanced by its relative rarity throughout the world. The granite outcrops of Devon and Cornwall with their veins of cassiterite, or tin oxide, constitute one of the very few sources of the metal in the whole of Europe. Despite the popular belief that tin from the mines of south-west England was exported by Phoenician merchants from the East Mediterranean, the earliest documented exploitation of Dartmoor tin deposits dates to the 13th century.

The earliest method of tin extraction, known as streaming, involved the digging out of tin ore bearing gravels on valley floors. Water has always played a significant part in the extraction of tin, not least in tin streaming. The erosive power of fast-running upland streams washed nuggets of tin ore from the lodes. The relatively high density of the ore caused it to settle in the valley floor, while less dense detritus was washed away downstream. Water power was also used in sorting the alluvial deposits: streams were diverted and small channels dug into alluvium deposits to allow the lighter material to be flushed away, leaving the tin ore. Additional water was collected and controlled for use in this process, and the remains of small reservoirs can be seen on the moor, marked by the low, curving dams. The floors of the Plym and its tributaries, including Drizzle Combe, all display evidence of tin streaming in the form of waste heaps of gravel. The steep sides of the valleys were the quarry faces at which the tin streamers worked.

The tin lodes on Dartmoor are aligned ENE-WSW, and once these were located, mining was possible. Some lodes were exploited by open-cast digging, which has left long, deep gullies following the orientation of the lode. The deeper lodes required the digging of vertical shafts. The numerous visible remains of Eylesbarrow Mine, which is also well-documented as having been in use from 1814 to 1852, exemplify the engineering skills which were necessary. The remains of many other mines, however, are now vestigial, and, with their machinery removed, they would be meaningless to the uninformed visitor.

The essential preoccupation of the miner was drainage. An adit, or tunnel, excavated horizontally from the side of the hill to meet the shaft, could drain the shallow levels of the mine. But deeper shafts required pumping by a device such as the rag and chain pump or the rod and piston. The pump was driven by a water wheel, and the power was transmitted by means of a flatrod system. A series of iron rods was joined together to form a single flat-rod, which might reach for more than a kilometre from the water wheel to the shaft. The only traces now to be seen are the pairs of granite stanchions, set at intervals of six or eight metres. Pulleys were set into grooves cut on the inner faces of the stanchions, and the iron rods were run over the pulleys.

The water for the water wheel was held in a reservoir and fed by a leat. From Langcombe Brook on the S. side of the River Plym a channel following the contour carried the water around the valley. The water supply was probably augmented by a leat which was carried across the Plym by a wooden conduit or launder. Over a distance of 4.5 kilometres the drop in height of the leat was only about 5 or 10 metres, but that was enough to ensure a free flow of water.

The water which had passed through the engine wheel house to drive the water wheel was not wasted. It was directed downhill for use in a series of dressing floors used in the processing of tin ore. The ore was first crushed in a stamping mill and then sorted in water. It was then ready to be sent for smelting. In the stamping mill a set of iron-shod wooden posts, called 'lifters', was set vertically in a row within a frame. They were lifted and let fall in sequence on the tin ore, which was retained in stone-built 'coffer'. The elutriation process, or sorting by water, was carried out in a series of rectangular, stone-lined pits. Today all that remains are the wheel-pits, the coffers, and traces of the buddles, or water- sorting pits.

Eylesbarrow was one of the few sites on Dartmoor where smelting was carried out at the place of extraction. The smelting house may have contained two types of furnace. The large, square, granite blocks at the W. end of the smelting house may be the remains of a blast furnace, in which ore was mixed with peat charcoal. The temperature was raised by a forced draught produced by water-powered bellows. A flue, or horizontal chimney, served to collect any tin particles which had escaped with the gas. The large blocks at the E. end of the building may be the remains of a reverbatory furnace, in which coal was used as the fuel. The different types of furnace produced different grades of tin, which would have been poured into granite moulds to produce ingots.

All that is left of this industrial complex, which was once a noisy, busy scene, are some of the stone structures. Thanks to the historical documentation and the contemporary illustrations, it will be possible to give the visitor to the Upper Plym Valley some idea, a faint echo, of the working of the tin industry. At the same time the visitors will be able to appreciate something of the traces in the landscape which tell of the old rabbit warreners, the medieval farmers and their remote, prehistoric forebears. A day in the quiet of Dartmoor will be enriched by learning something of the various ways in which the people of past generations once inhabited and earned their livelihoods in what is now one of the least populated parts of the country.

Balfarg henge, Glenrothes, Fife, Scotland

In a field close to the farmhouse of Balfarg stood two standing stones, all that was left to be seen of what archaeologists believed to be a lost prehistoric stone circle and ritual enclosure. The form of the buried ditch of the henge enclosure had been noted as a dark crop-mark on an aerial photograph but there was no trace on the surface. As the new town of Glenrothes grew and spread it became clear that there was a potential conflict between the ancient site and the housing development for which the field was zoned.

The proposed solution was a rescue excavation of the henge. Though there are many stone circles, very few of the circular ritual enclosures which we call henges are known in Scotland. The excavation would recover the surviving information from the obviously badly damaged, four thousand year old stone circle, and the site could then be turned over to the housing development.

As the excavation progressed and the site slowly revealed more and more quite unexpected details of its long history of construction and reconstruction, Glenrothes Development Corporation began to think again. In the end the plans of that part of the new town were re-drawn, and the area of the henge and stone circle were left as an open recreation area. The funds were found to landscape the area, reconstruct elements of the monument, and provide an interpretation of the site in the form of a printed leaflet and an information plaque on the site.

The huge, almost circular ditch with its accompanying bank on its outer side was delineated on the ground by scooping part of the fill out of the ditch. The henge ditch as excavated was massively deep, and could not have been safely left open; also, for the sake of easy maintenance and soil stability the whole surface had to be grassed. The excavations had revealed that in its original form the interior of the henge had accumulated six concentric rings of large timber posts, which had been replaced by a broad circle of standing stones. Only two of the stones had survived to this century, and they were put back in their settings after having been removed while the excavation took place. One of the circles of wooden posts was reconstructed in the interior, and the stone-lined cist-grave which had been found at the very centre of the monument was put back with its capstone firmly locked in place.

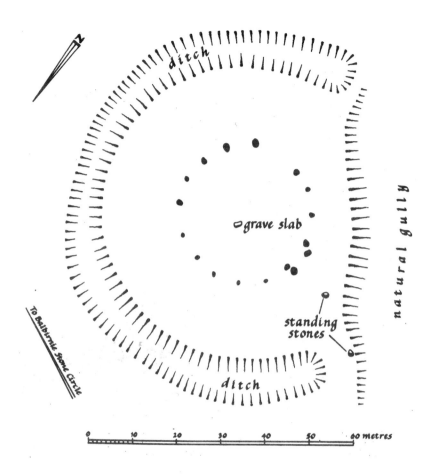

Fig 28. The simplified plan of Balfarg henge as reconstructed at Glenrothes, Fife

Glenrothes has added a charming epilogue to the story of Balfarg. When a traffic roundabout was inserted into the road junction where one turns off the main road to visit Balfarg henge, the town commissioned its sculptor-in-residence to erect an appropriate monument on it. Obviously impressed by the curious conjunction of the ancient henge in the middle of the modern town, he has erected a massive circle of synthetic monoliths to produce Britain's only hengiform traffic island.

List of illustrations

A puzzler's guide to further clues

Part 1. New projects with no further published references.

Aerial survey in Scotland.
Bowmont Valley, S.E. Scotland.
Early settlement in the Outer Hebrides
Wear analysis on chipped stone tools
Bronze weapons of the ancient Levant
Beads and bowdrills, Jordan
Farming experiments, Callanish, Outer Hebrides, Scotland
Ritual and its paraphernalia, Mosphilia, Cyprus
Diatom analysis
The ancient city of Ed-Dur, United Arab Emirates
Portable computers for on-site data-capture
New ways to publication
Upper Plym Valley, Devon; landscape interpretation

Part 2. Further references to research projects

The Black Desert, Jordan
> BETTS, A. V. G. The Black Desert Survey. Prehistoric sites and subsistence strategies in eastern Jordan. In A. N. Garrard and H. G. Gebel (eds.), The Prehistory of Jordan in 1986. British Archaeological Reports (International Series), Oxford 1987.

Wadi al Qawr, Ras al-Khaimah, United Arab Emirates
> PHILLIPS, C. S., Wadi al Qawr, Fashga 1. The Excavation of a prehistoric burial structure in Ras al Khaimah, U. A. E., 1986. University of Edinburgh, Department of Archaeology, Project Paper No.7. 1987

Eskmeals, Cumbria, N.W. England
> BONSALL, C. et al. 'The Eskmeals Project 1981-5: an interim report.' Northern Archaeology 7, part 1 (1986).

Mosphilia, S.W. Cyprus
> PELTENBURG, E. J. et al. Excavations at Kissonerga Mosphilia, 1985-6. Report of the Department of Antiquities, Cyprus, 1986-87.

Newmill, Perthshire, Scotland
> WATKINS, T., Excavation of a settlement and souterrain at Newmill, near Bankfoot, Perthshire. Proc. Soc. Antiq, Scot 110 (1980), 165-208

Inveresk, Mid Lothian, Scotland
    THOMAS, G. D. Excavations at the Roman civil settlement of
    Inveresk. Proc. Soc. Antiq. Scot. 117 (forthcoming).

Carn Brea, Cornwall, England
    MERCER, R. J. Excavations at Carn Brea, Illogan, Cornwall,
    1970-73; a neolithic fortified complex of the third millennium
    b.c. Truro. 1971

Hambledon Hill, Dorset, England
    MERCER, R. J. Hambledon Hill: a neolithic landscape.
    Edinburgh. 1980

Green Castle, Portknockie, Grampian, Scotland
    RALSTON, I. B. M., Portknockie: promontory forts and
    pictish settlement in the North-East. In A. Small (ed.), The
    Picts: a new look at old problems. Dundee. 1987

Levroux and Mont Beuvray, France
    COLLIS, J. Oppida: Earliest Towns North of the Alps.
    Sheffield. 1984

Grimes Graves flint mines, Norfolk, England
    MERCER, R. J. Grimes Graves Norfolk: Excavations 1971-72. 2
    vols, H.M.S.O. 1981

The early technology of glass
    PELTENBURG, E. J. Early faience: recent studies, origins and
    relations with glass. In M. Bunson and I. Freestone (eds.),
    Early Vitreous Material, London 1987.

Fingerprinting clays to map the potters' markets
    WATKINS, T. & CAMPBELL, S. Kharabeh Shattani 1983.
    University of Edinburgh, Department of Archaeology,
    Occasional Papers No. , 1986

Reconstructing the Balbridie building, Deeside, Scotland
    RALSTON, I. B. M. Balbridie. Aberdeen University Press.
    1982

Reconstructing a cist-grave, Dalgety, Fife
    McADAM, E. & WATKINS, T., Experimental rconstruction of
    a short cist. J. of Archaeol. Sci. 1 (1975), 383-6

Vitrified ramparts, the burning question
RALSTON, I. B. M. The Yorkshire Television vitrified wall experiment at East Tullos, City of Aberdeen. Proc. Soc. Antiq. Scot. 116 (forthcoming).

Barns Farm cemetery, Dalgety, Fife, Scotland
WATKINS, T. The excavation of an Early Bronze Age cemetery at Barns Farm, Dalgety, Fife. Proc. Soc. Antiq. Scot. 112 (1982), 48-141

Long burial mounds of North Europe
MIDGLEY, M. S. The Origin and Function of the Earthen Long Barrows of Northern Europe. British Archaeological Reports (International Series 259), Oxford 1985.

Rites of death at Hambledon Hill, Dorset, England
See under project 13 above.

The society of Pithekoussai, Ischia, Italy
RIDGWAY, D. W., L'Alba della Magna Grecia. Milan, 1984

Rullion Green, Mid Lothian, Scotland
WATKINS, T. Rullion Green: report on the 1983 season of excavations. University of Edinburgh, Department of Archaeology, Project Paper No.1, 1984 (Similarly the report on the 1984 season forms Project Paper No.3, 1985.)

Rock art in the Jordanian desert.
BETTS, A. V. G. The hunter's perspective: 7th millennium B.C. rock carvings from eastern Jordan. World Archaeology 19/2 (1987), 214-224.

Caithness marginal land survey, Scotland
MERCER, R. J. Archaeological Field Survey in Northern Scotland, Volumes 1, 2 & 3. University of Edinburgh, Department of Archaeology, Occasional Papers Nos. 4, 7 & 11.

Eski Mosul Dam Salvage Archaeology Project, N. Iraq
See under Project 20 above.

Balfarg henge, Glenrothes, Fife, Scotland
MERCER, R. J. The excavation of a late Neolithic henge-type enclosure at Balfarg, Markinch, Fife. Proc. Soc. Antiq. Scot 111 (1981), 63-171.